THE BEST BRITISH POETRY

2014

◇　◇　◇

Mark Ford was born in 1962 in Nairobi, Kenya. He has published four volumes of poetry, *Landlocked* (1992), *Soft Sift* (2001), *Six Children* (2011) and *Selected Poems* (2014), and three collections of essays. He has also written a biography of the French poet, playwright and novelist Raymond Roussel, and translated Roussel's *New Impressions of Africa*. His anthology *London: A History in Verse* was published in 2012. He is a regular contributor to the *London Review of Books* and the *New York Review of Books*. He teaches in the English Department at University College London.

Roddy Lumsden (born 1966) is a Scottish poet, who was born in St Andrews. He has published six collections of poetry, a number of chapbooks and a collection of trivia, as well as editing a generational anthology of British and Irish poets of the 1990s and 2000s, *Identity Parade*. He lives in London where he teaches for The Poetry School. He has done editing work on several prize-winning poetry collections and edited the Pilot series of chapbooks by poets under 30 for tall-lighthouse. He is organiser and host of the monthly reading series BroadCast in London. In 2010, he was appointed as Poetry Editor for Salt.

Jon Stone was born in Derby and currently lives in Whitechapel. He's the co-creator of pocket poetry journal *Fuselit* and micro-anthology publishers Sidekick Books. He was highly commended in the National Poetry Competition 2009, the same month his debut pamphlet, *Scarecrows* (Happenstance), was released. His debut collection *School of Forgery* was published by Salt in 2012.

THE
BEST
BRITISH
POETRY

2014

◇   ◇   ◇

Mark Ford, *Editor*
Roddy Lumsden, *Series Editor*

with Jon Stone

SALT

CROMER

PUBLISHED BY SALT

12 Norwich Road, Cromer, Norfolk NR27 0AX United Kingdom

Printed in Great Britain by Clays Ltd, St Ives plc

Typeset in Bembo 10.5 / 12

ISBN 978 1 907773 68 6 paperback

1 3 5 7 9 8 6 4 2

CONTENTS

FOREWORD

by Roddy Lumsden

◊ ◊ ◊

The poems presented in this volume were selected from UK-based poetry magazines, literary journals and online publications issued between spring 2014 and spring 2014. The main purpose of this volume is to celebrate the thriving scene of literary magazines and the developing sphere of literary sites online. For the past twelve months, this year's Guest Editor Mark Ford has been reading these publications as they appeared, seeking poems which he felt should be reproduced here. The format of the book owes a debt to *The Best American Poetry* series of anthologies which was founded in 1988. Similar volumes appear each year in Canada, Australia and Ireland. I would like to offer many thanks to the poet Jon Stone, who steered the collation of this year's anthology during a time when I had health problems.

INTRODUCTION

by Mark Ford

◇   ◇   ◇

For some poets, the business of reading, assessing, and then deciding whether to print or not to print the work of their contemporaries is a daily activity. Publishers' poetry lists and poetry magazines are, by and large, edited by other poets, although there have been exceptions such as Charles Monteith, whose notable signings for Faber & Faber included Philip Larkin and Seamus Heaney, and Robert Giroux of the New York firm Farrar Straus Giroux. Giroux once asked Monteith's famous predecessor, T.S. Eliot, poet-editor par excellence, if he agreed that most editors were failed writers, to which the Pope of Russell Square coolly replied: 'Perhaps, but so are most writers.'

Not being a poet-editor, I had some difficulty sorting out in my mind what kind of criteria to apply to the cornucopia of poems I set about weighing in the balance. What would Milton or Tennyson make of this poem? was one particularly futile question I found myself asking. In the end, probably like most editors, I just went on my nerve: a poem rings one's bell, or it doesn't; or it almost does, but then it doesn't quite; or it doesn't look like it's going to, but wasn't that last line quite good? A possible? Photocopy it anyway . . . Making my way through all the poems published in magazines and ezines between May 2013 and May 2014 in the hush of the Saison Poetry Library on level 5 of the Royal Festival Hall, I kept thinking of football stadiums: if one could gather all the poets currently writing and publishing in English, would they fill, say, Old Trafford? Yes, easily, surely. One of the most bracing effects of being entrusted with the editing of this volume is the awareness it engenders of the bewildering number and variety of poets currently at work. Has there ever been a time when so much poetry was written and published by so many?

I haven't been able to represent every strand of our poetic nation, and haven't time in this brief introduction to offer any sort of taxonomy of the kinds of poetry filling these magazines and ezines. Possibly a software programme could crunch and plot them; or, better, an eloquent critic with an interest in British poetry will emerge with a convincing and compelling account of what is interesting about the poetry being written in the twenty-first century. It is odd that there is so little good literary criticism that deals with contemporary poetry, about which there is surely plenty to say. There are reviews, of course, but these too tend to be the work of other poets.

Paul Muldoon once described an anthologist as a 'despot' whose introduction then serves to justify his or her despotism as 'reasonable and benevolent'. While searching out poems for this volume, I felt more like a fish catching glimpses of other fish whose stripes or colours or speed I admired. But as Muldoon implies, whatever analogy one uses, there is in the end not much more justification to offer than personal taste and inclination. I believe that the poems assembled here make a good book, and with that assertion will rest my case.

THE
BEST
BRITISH
POETRY
2014

◇ ◇ ◇

MIG-21 *Raids at Shegontola*

◇ ◇ ◇

Only this boy moves
between the runes of trees
on his tricycle
when an eagle swoops,
releases two arrows
from its silver wings and melts
away faster than lightning.
Then a loud whistle
and a bang like dry thunder.
In a blink the boy sees
his house roof sink.
Feels his ears ripped off.
The blast puffs up a fawn smoke
bigger than a mountain cloud.
The slow begonias rattle
their scarlet like confetti.
Metal slashes
the trees and ricochets.
Wires and pipes snap
at the roots, quiver.
The whirling smoke packed
with bricks and cement,
chicken feathers and nigella seeds.
When the cloud begins
to settle on the ground,
the boy makes out buckled iron rods.
White soot descends
and he finds himself dressed
like an apprentice baker.

from *Poetry Review*

Science and Math

/sci/

◊ ◊ ◊

Dear Mr Mitchell and Mrs Snell
Sorry for drawing upside
down triangles in the back of my exercise books and turning
them into the most angular nude women with tufty bottoms and
circle breasts I promise that I was doing my best to balance
something or other against the state of stress at the points
against something

the thing is
my mother would step out of the bath each evening unashamed
and frosted with bubbles and even though her body was my
body I was yet to see these rings of flesh as mine she was so
heat-speckled

so at the same time as
clumsy fresh boys were fizzing hair on the Bunsen burner I was
debating what of mine would fill the planet-sized bra on the
landing and when

from *Poetry London*

ROBERT ANTHONY

Clouds

◊   ◊   ◊

They gather in parties of vapour, big swirling get-togethers
that are like clubs with smoke machines without the club.
The clouds mingle, they make their own darkness
– we may imagine them taping up the windows of their squat,
so that the mood darkens, gets gothy, and the night starts right now –
they can turn on the strobes. Lightning!
They crash around and fight.

Later, they break up and go their own ways,
some of them soothing down to earth, cooling off in a Jamaican waterfall,
some of them pushing the neurotic buttons of a Welsh poet,
steady rain, cold against the slate.
Sometimes they end up stuck in bad relationships with the empty cold
and remain, long after the whole thing has gone bad,
trapped under miles of ice in a flat in Antarctica, what have you.

Everything they own is wet, moist with mildew.
Their hugs are half-hearted and empty.
On the most beautiful days they are alone and separate:
floating high in a crisp summer day, they are too far apart
to comment on the breathtaking scenery.
Only in bad weather do they get together,
crammed tight like commuters.

In the end they all crave the desert,
missionary work where they know they'll be appreciated,
something to give their life meaning.
When they arrive they are eaten by the natives,
sucked deep into the sand and held there by roots and worms,

their corpse-water treasured by the most powerful plants and chieftains,
their water-skeletons powerful totems in the sun.

from *Kaffeeklatsch*

Emergency

◇ ◇ ◇

The four-pump petrol garage
finally closed,
its defeated owner
inhaling his ghost
in a disused quarry
by coupling the lips of his car exhaust
to the roots of his lungs
via a garden hose;

on the bulldozed forecourt
they threw up a tram-shed
for decommissioned emergency vehicles
where a skeleton workforce
service all manneration
of mothballed workhorses
for occasional call-outs
to sitcoms, period-dramas and film sets.

And the actual fire-station's
up for rent,
that chapel-shaped building
where they stabled the one engine,
spit-buffing and wire-woolling
the chrome fenders,
T-Cutting the steel coachwork
to a flame red.

So what you see,
as the letting-agent puts it,
is what you get:
boot-cupboard, functional kitchenette,
brass hooks – two still holding

a brace of yolk-yellow plastic helmets –
northlight roof-windows
and inspection pit.

The makeshift crew
were volunteer part-timers:
butchers, out-menders,
greasy perchers and hill-farmers
who'd pitch up in bloody aprons,
boiler suits or pyjamas
then venture forth,
fire-slaying on the tender.

Sometimes in dreams
my fire-fighting forefathers
appear, alien-like,
breathing from oxygen cylinders
through a sudden parting
of towering, black cumulonimbus
on fully telescoped
turntable ladders.

The bank's gone as well,
and also the post office,
though in the store-cum-off-licence
you can sign a gyro
with a string-and-sellotape-tethered
half-chewed biro
or deface a scratch-card
or sell a bullmastiff.

The horizon ablaze –
is it moor-fire or sundown?
In the local taproom
prescription jellies and tin-foil wraps
change hands under cover
of *Loot* magazine
and Tetley beer mats.
What is it we do now?

from *The New Statesman*

MICHAEL BAYLEY

Estuary

after Graham Sutherland

◊   ◊   ◊

The exultant strangeness
      of this place
           for strange it certainly is.
Many people hate it,
      and I admit
           it possesses an element
of disquiet; the whole
      setting one of
           exuberance, of darkness
and light: the life-
      giving sound
           of the mechanical reaper;
cattle crouching
      among the gorse;
           a horse's skull or horns
of cattle, lying bleached
      on the sand.
           And now as the tide
recedes, the black-
      green ribs
           of half-buried wrecks,
phantom tree-roots
      whitened
           to bone by the waves.

from *Poetry Wales*

7

FIONA BENSON

Toboggan Run

◊ ◊ ◊

Midnight, early February. Moonlight – trapped
between the snow still falling and the white earth –
is luminous from our sloped roof to the firs
that edge the common land. In the white curve

of the field beyond, figures almost drowned
in the static interference of snow and distance
toboggan down the spills. They're so far off,
so dimly seen – a black speck riding the cataracts

and screes of our deepest snowfall in years.
Their runners leave the snow-warp as they leap,
like animals possessed beyond their strength –
spawning salmon, startled deer. What would I give

to be one of those swimmers in all this snow,
swallowed by the cold and the night's strange radiance?
Would I leave this house, its synthesis of brightness,
would I give myself to the wind? The snow pulls a veil

across the moonlit world, deepens and draws in
on figures lost to the year's last blizzard,
tobogganing a swerving run through our rarest weather,
on and on, liturgy or evensong or requiem for snow.

from *Granta*

Picnic

◊　◊　◊

If you are not happy, the sea is not happy
It sulks in and out of the bay
I lie on the bed or stand at the window watching the sea
Why must we destroy what we do
Watching the sea is like watching something in pieces continually
　　　striving to be whole
Imagine trying to pick up a piece of the sea and show it to a person
I tried to do that
All that year I visited a man in a room
I polished my feelings
Sometimes I think if the devil came and offered to swap me into some
　　　other body without me knowing what I'd be getting, I'd say . . . *Sure*
And, sure, I believe in the devil

I wanted to love the world
I thought when all the anxiety slipped away, I'd watch it go, and I'd know
　　　precisely
Every increment of its departure
The way 'getting better' can be an unfolding
The covers pulled back, the light coming in

★

　　The mood of the sea is catching
Your eyes wear out from all the glitches
I sat there watching it and I can assure you it is so
Its colour became the colour of my eyes and the salt made me cry oceans

★

I like curved things
　　Apples, peaches, the crest of a wave

We once agreed the apple was the only iconic fruit

I like it when I am writing a poem and I know that I am feeling
      something
To be poised and to invite contact
Or to appear to invite contact

> *Remember when we used to imagine*
> *Our correspondence would make us famous or that*
> *Once we'd become famous our correspondence would too?*
> *Maybe it still will*
> *I'll need to make a lot of cuts first*

When did everybody start wanting to be famous all the time
Or has it always been this way
This is the rain, the October rain
I wrote that when it was still October
It must have been raining

This is sadness: men in waterproofs dragging the deep lake
The warm American voice says: *There is no lack or limitation, there is only*
      error in thought
My thoughts are wrong. My thoughts are wrong
The thought that my thoughts are wrong is wrong

★

I started to be able to see in the dark
It hurt my eyes
           My, yes, salty, wet, ocean-coloured eyes
Albeit that in the dark they were the colour of the dark, and on fire

★

When the rain came after the drought they said it was not good enough
It would not change things
It was the wrong rain
The rain came out of my eyes and fell on the ground and dried up
I achieved no *release*

Who are you. Who are you. Who are you

Stop, language is crawling all over me

Sometimes if you stay still long enough you can make it go
If a person standing still watched another person minutely moving
    would it seem after a while as if they were watching the sea?
I remember just one thing my mother said to me:
Never look at yourself in the mirror when you're crying
    I did not follow her advice

from *Granta*

Scenes from The Passion
– *The First Path*

◊　◊　◊

When you found me there was nothing beautiful about me.
I wasn't even human
                              just a mongrel
kicked out into the snow on Maundy Thursday
when all the world was sorrow,
when old girls' hands were raw as they cracked
the ice on their birdbaths,
when the priest wept in Saint Jude the Apostle
as he knelt to wash the feet of an altar boy.

I was filth,
            running away from God knows what,
my haunches sore with bruises,
my spine knuckling the ruin of my coat.

Running through the town
                              away from the horses
who bowed their heads to the donkey-bite,
away from the boy in the bus shelter
                              who turned from me
to receive a snowflake
like a wafer on his tongue.

Lord help me
                  I did things I would once
have been ashamed of.

Now no-one would come near me,
                              they feared
the hunger that gnawed and whined in my bones,

the hurt I would carry into their houses.

Only you dared follow
                              upon the track
of my bloodied paw prints in the ice,
where the trees held snow in their arms
like winding sheets.
                              You came for me there
                                        close, low,
calling a name that was not mine.
Calling *wench, my wench*
as the tongues of the church bells rang mute.

At your scent on the air,
                              I shot
through the woods – a grey cry –
so raw only the dusk could touch me

but you were patient,
                              waited
through the dense muffled hours
until darkness dropped and I sank into the midden
behind the factory
and the chimneys cast a wreath of ash upon me.

          You touched me then,
                    when I was nothing but dirt,
took off your glove and laid your palm upon my throat,
slipped the loop of the rope,

                    lifted me
into your arms and carried me home
                                        along the first path.

In the banks the foxes barked *alleluia alleluia*.

The blizzard tumbled upon us like confetti
and I, little bitch, blue bruise,
saw myself in your eyes:
                              a bride.

from *Poetry Review*

13

RACHAEL BOAST

The North Porch

(Thomas Chatterton)

◊　◊　◊

Not knowing until the moment comes
at some late hour, who you are,
or might be; raving in the Lunacy

of Ink, the night tapering, dissimilated
from papyrus, from scraps, from daily bread;
the three-fold bosses of tail chasing tail

after tail; looking out at the gospel
in capitals, level with the buttresses,
led back, time and again, to the image,

not of the builder but of his masonry;
of dream-vision, miraculous city,
the marvelous breasts of the girls in the doorway . . .

from *Edinburgh Review*

ALAN BROWNJOHN

Index of First Lines

◊   ◊   ◊

Randomly, sleet that night becoming snow,
Requests you merely me, but hugged demands
Rudderless, our slow craft surely
Sex can be relevant – *But the thing to learn*
Single departures. One by one, leaving
Somewhere the one green county your
Take care was all their advice, who never
Tell me again, Eurydice, what should I
Undertows and underworlds
Vanity Fair came high on a shaming list
Velvet feet took ten steps. His leap, an arc
'We understand your wishes, but can't grant
X meaning *Extra Size*, not the Spot where
You were not there to praise the play, I thought
Z, z, zed, noun, twenty-sixth and last

from the *Times Literary Supplement*

COLETTE BRYCE

Don't speak to the Brits, just pretend they don't exist

Two rubber bullets stand on the shelf,
from Bloody Sunday – mounted in silver,

space rockets docked and ready to go off;
like the Sky Ray Lolly that crimsons your lips

when the orange Quencher your brother gets
attracts a wasp that stings him on the tongue.

'Tongue' is what they call the Irish language,
'native tongue' you're learning at school.

Kathleen is sent home from the Gaeltacht
for speaking English, and it's there

at the Gaeltacht, ambling back
along country roads in pure darkness

that a boy from Dublin
talks his tongue right into your mouth,

holds you closely in the dark and calls it
French kissing (he says this in English).

from *Edinburgh Review*

Choir

◊　◊　◊

I think, if I tried, I could go back and sing again
no worse than I did at twelve, when my voice broke too soon
and I moved to the back of the choir on practice days,
mouthing the words and hoping that no one would hear
the missing soprano.
I stayed for the sudden dark at the stained glass window,
the sense of a vigil it gave me, like waiting for snow
at the presbytery door, a shape stealing in from the cold
to claim me for some lost kingdom; I stayed for the candles
and, off to the side of the altar, the theatre of absence
that made more sense, to me,
than our Sunday School God.

Close to retirement, the choirmaster hammered away
at the upright piano,
not for a moment
deceived, so much
in tune with us, he knew each voice by name,
the way a herdsman knows his animals:
the Cunningham twins, their faces so alike
that no one could tell them apart, until they sang;
the Polish boy, Marek; the grammar school beauty who smelled
like cinnamon after the rain
– he knew us all by heart, each voice he heard
combining with every child he had taught to sing
through a lifetime of choir, so thoroughly rehearsed
he swore he would pick us out
on Judgment Day.

I turned up every week for six months more;
and all that time he kept
my secret, each of us

pretending not to know the other knew.
I mouthed the words; he played; nobody guessed,
or everyone did; it doesn't matter now.
Later I switched to blues and The Rolling Stones,
Mandies and cider, Benzedrine, Lebanese;
so, though I wanted to, I couldn't
make it to Our Lady's on the day
they buried him next to his wife, in the steeltown rain,
to prepare for the Second Coming; and anyway,
despite the years of Kyries and hymns,
I never quite saw the point
of the life to come; back then it seemed
that, like as not, most everything runs on
as choir: all one; the living and the dead:
first catch, then canon; fugal; *all one breath*.

from the *London Review of Books*

A Prism of Signs

◇ ◇ ◇

Latency: Present but not visible, apparent,
or actualised. Existing as potential.

I remember sitting after dark, grubbed in oak-smoke
        and rabbit grease

listening to my father   reeling them off – Leshy
        Waldtgeist, Alhool –

until his eyes dimmed with memory and he refused
        to go on.

Lore I: Offering

Separate the weakest infants. Sew them into their
rowan and cuckoo spit cots and place them on the
border of dusk. Return to the relative safety of the
trees, and wait for the ragged clank of its breath.

And now   standing at the hinge of wood and sky
        after the mutt-pack

eager and slavering for fox has passed on   we sense
        in the sudden hackling

of neck hair, something not seen   but known
        watching us

from beyond the scrub line.   With our long guns
                    and our catalogue of myth

we find ourselves   after it, past the hollow of grass
                    where it had lain

and smouldered, past a bark stripped tree   where
                    something less than animal

            had flexed up and sculpted it's claws.

Lore II: Masking

In the half-light that occupies all forests, wash the
dead clean. Take a cut of your spleen, and with it:
sew together the mauve flab of their gums. Cleave
ground. Cut down to the earth's granite bone. Fill
the flesh with fire until it hums.

We walk on   finding more of its muzzle prints –
                    snagged wool

and blood, a roe-buck left unburied   in the sky
                    and a set of tracks

that come into view then vanish   where something
                    has been   hawked up.

Night comes. It fits around us like a glove   and still
                    there is nothing

save the swelter of trunk gloom   and the moonlight
                    raising the woods grain.

Lore III: Deceit

Take one dying colt. Stitch your sweat into its mane.
Farrier its hooves with your skin. Return home.
Smear pheasant shit over the lintel. Bolt the dogs in
the wood-shed. Clamp up like fists. Pray.

The world opens at dawn. We step out of ourselves
            to where a battery of rain

is no longer drawn across the moors   as a harbinger
            and there   in front of us –

our own shadows   caught for a moment on
            the kissing gate ahead.

from *Poetry Wales*

from *The Victor Poems*

◊   ◊   ◊

1. *The path*

The sea is melting into floes.

The melt-water softens our dogs' paws and ice splinters their
toes.

We tie seal-skin boots they try to flick off.

We sled the ice-foot, the belt of shore-fast, until the air is as
crass as the water below.

The ground is patched brown like our faces.

We stand with knees tucked, bent-backed until the wind blows
thin willows slack against the sky.

Who is happier than us to be alive?

It's easy to see the copse as a corpse – but trees are trees.

Give us breath or give us death, Victor!

We struggle through the willows till they become the pines
we've had in our mind for some time.

Snow mixes with dirt – bare-black.

The mountains behind us slip away flat-packed.

We walk a path of flowers pale and pink until we hear Victor
in the trees, ready to fall like snow.

Under our feet the flowers crack, blue as glass.

Under our feet, the dogs circle, the shadows of birds circle.

A change in the wind is a change in our luck.

Uncovered a rusty chainsaw, an orange . . .

2. *The path, continued*

. . . truck.

The path in front of us is part muck, part shuck of engines.

A two-stroke engine with a problem confronts us.

We can't fix a two-stroke anymore than we can fix a four-
stroke.

A wet spark plug, someone says, can mean many things.

A wet dream, we say, can mean many things.

The sparks look lost, weak, slack-jawed.

The path doesn't crash – but it has a weak chin, a smash-
through-the-windshield sort-of-grin.

We'd smile if it didn't hurt.

From over our shoulders one of our huskies lolls an oil-black
tongue: Check the ground wire for the ignition coil.

The gas line sprays and we're on our knees praying for a spark.

A path is its own catheter, Victor.

Rewire the hope in our hearts with the veins in our legs.

Any minute now we expect you to step out of the fog like one
of our dogs with a wrench, whacking pistons:

tick

tick

ping.

We're high on the smell of smoke that fills the sky.

Not from behind, but ahead.

Burning dwarf willow and heather, from a camp above the
weather.

from *The Manchester Review*

The thing about Grace and Laura

◊　◊　◊

was that they were sisters, *vice versas*.
The gentleness of the one, tender
as mousse, flesh like marshmallow;
her demeanour like Turkish Delight;
an apricot mooning
at the sun; a salve for sore *I*.

The gunmetal slickness of the other,
her flick-knife wit and belt-buckle
tongue; operating from offices
in the City. I couldn't love
her. A wildcat, out of
control, she stalked me through winters.

Grace slides laughing on her birthday,
her soft haunches streaked with yellow
from tiger-lilies I've placed on her path.
Laura sucks in her cheeks and
intimates that, as per her email,
she won't be celebrating
anything in the current climate.

I edge away from her
coat-hanger glance.

If Grace and Laura were to marry,
that would be incest, anathema.
I covet a calling card for Grace
and she is always welcome.
Laura has me poked to bits
with reminders; red letters.

from *Shearsman*

Desk

A cento

◊   ◊   ◊

Dressed to kill or inflict a wound,
in the reading chair, like one of the saved, white blossoms open on my
     fingertips.

There were others to whom she would have talked,
the part-Cherokee teenage genius (maybe).

Rain. The weather has turned. It will do that.
The sky is dark.

Light falls outside of my window on the red brick planes,
and I almost glimpse

her father in the camps of Moldova –
a man so easily distracted.

He rises in the small hours, finds a book
burning.

from *Poetry London*

Chekhov's Gun

◊ ◊ ◊

From a train, she passes how all things pass, wrapped
in their instants, messy and simple as the as-yet unlooked-at

complication, under the sign for a rail station named Marsden –
which is like the surname of a first love, from

before I understood, like now – standing alone,
the inscrutable woman, all cheekbones

and short hair, and red polkadots rapped onto their white,
her hand raised to rest – perhaps briefly – against her cheek. Life,

for Chekhov, is neither horrible, nor happy,
but strange, unique, fleeting, beautiful and awful, according to
        Gerhardie

in this book I was reading before I shot by and saw the lee
of the sign for Marsden. And for me, also – and for me.

from *Poems in Which*

Big Cats

◇ ◇ ◇

Unpuncture the hens' bellies, please. Bring them back unstunned,
intact, still glad and laying large eggs.

But this is not the work of foxes. This is tidy, even careful,
kind. See, no blood. No scattered feathers or scuffle.

So what do you figure went this way, leaving behind it,
a whole fence and a locked gate but
no Frizzle Hens or Naked Necks?
What put a paw on ruffled feathers last night?

Search the woods for it, scale the rocks if you must.
Walk miles and get lost. They say it has whiskers,
a black back and prints as big as boulders. It knows you
like the land does: your weight, your footsteps,
your greasy hair runs through the air in tart tracks.
It feels you ten tree trunks ahead – the something out there,
beyond what we know. Maybe I like it –
not knowing what pads about our walls at night.
What I know is this: we're left with
nothing. Nothing but crusty shit and straw stuck to cold eggs.
Shells clack in our fingers in the morning as we look them over,
deep-scratched earth and old squats on grass,
full water bowls, and you,
calling louder and louder,
calling the vanished to breakfast.

from *Poetry Wales*

a glass of ice cold milk

◊　◊　◊

The nubile sky bit her lip and rolled suggestively onto her stomach yet there was snow in February, and taxes. The ornamental grammar of thought persisted, unreal and perfect. Besides, posterity may explain all this as having nothing to do with us and acquit us entirely, chalking it up to something which happened long ago, perhaps in another country, or something somebody said in another country. We must of course accept backward steps as being part of the healing process. The stitches will unravel.

The doctor will perch like a great white bird in his white cap and mask, scalpel poised, over the anesthetised patient on the operating table and fight his silent bout with the mystery. The wind howls. The great butcher moon stands proud as punch in his big fancy shop.

Wee critters root about the rhododendrons and make plans for the future. How long have we wrestled with the prescription in the awful water, shedding mysteries like petals, only to finally find the thing suddenly obscured by a darned concrete pillar or some such, waking from a deep sleep to be abruptly brought to tears by a cruel story or a sentimental tune, merely to fall back into a deep deep sleep? Once all the village was laid out like a dinner table, the houses napkins folded in fancy shapes, the truth shining.

They lived in an orchard in the summer and autumn, batting down the crispy fruit with wooden swords and munching their way through some of their bounty. Green food was popularly believed to be poisonous. The men wore bonnets. When they grew old they made noodles from the bark of the trees and were placed in front of big brick fireplaces. Perhaps our mandate

was never to dream hard wintry dreams but is rather how to weigh the ration of light the next day would bring, if anything? Come back to bed for a while longer and let me kiss your lovely bottom for a bit before I have to leave, for I unexpectedly find myself the beleaguered warden of a moody tower – the tower of passion.

from *Kaffeeklatsch*

Skype Blinks

◇　◇　◇

Everyone is moving away
and we are all now becoming
ventriloquists.

We are misdirecting eye contact,
impossible to tell where to focus
on the seconded face,
where we can connect.

I watched the sun rise
through the windows
of an apartment in South Korea

and thought I could hear
the 5am inflections in your voice
but this is taken on trust.

The way your dawn settled
on our dusk audience, the morning storm refracted
through unfamiliar windows
pinned my pupils to the glass.

Think about this specific drift,
and faces, numerous
failings, glitch in the tongue –

I am seeking completeness you said.
We applaud the wall.

I feel a sensation in the body I can't place
unbalancing –

and then abruptly we are talking about
polar bears' relationship to containment
and it made sense as a whole –

how the image is undesirable
singular and starving
let loose on the vast ice shelf

when fishing is merely a pastime in the cell
and the keeper lets us sleep
as much as we like.

Beneath the window prisms
each distracted orb precisely overlaps
in constellations.

The polar bear beside his limited pool
denies his reflection in the shallows,
while our own peripheries flicker,
fractional handles of light.

from 3:*AM Magazine*

The Terns

After Rebecca Horn

◇ ◇ ◇

Through that night when we nearly let go
we kept a lamp burning, ribboning the walls
with shadows as if waiting for light to untie us,
to unfasten something within.

Your hands were birds. They knew the earth
as a passing thing, an existence below,
and they lifted their dark feathers to it, confidently,
the way love would never be.

My hair was the place for owls.
It held their moon-pulled bodies in its crown
of moss and straw, their fat eyes swallowing
the darkness, heads turning for what lay behind.

What they saw was this; morning
hefting our lives against the terns, their wings
peeling back the fig-purple dawn as they made for air,
for a sky we couldn't touch.

from *Days of Roses*

RICHARD EVANS

Space Invader

after Dan Rhodes

◊   ◊   ◊

The first
time we met,
my wife invaded my space.
She stood uncomfortably close, listening intently
to my conversation. When I backed away, she followed.
We completed a rhumba across the floor, until I was backed against the
freezer in the corner. (There was nowhere else to run). Even at the wedding
as we spoke   our vows,   her nose   was awkwardly
close to mine: no backing   out now   I thought.
Now I have grown used to her presence
and that
of her equally
space invading parents, and friends.
I feel less   threatened than I did.   I feel
we   are
very   close.

from *Magma*

The Motorway

◇　◇　◇

I was born in the motorway era:
we both were. He used to say it made him
happy to see me writing in the car,
in the passenger seat.

We drove the motorways – going north on
the M1, all the routes through France heading south,
west from Nashville to San Diego, then
east again across the continent
to Montauk Point before returning the car:
you driving, me writing.

Sometimes I'd be aware you'd quickly turned
your head sideways, only for a moment
shifting your gaze from the road – one flick
of your eyes, to watch me making notes.
I laughed and said: 'It's perfect – you driving,
me writing, let's go on like this forever',
and you laughed and agreed.

But we didn't. There were other things to do.
And now it's impossible. You're dead.
And I'm driving with another person,
with someone else.

I stare through the windscreen into the distance
as the pylons draw their lines of power
across the green and brown and yellow fields,
the landscape of small hills, hedges and streams
you taught me to understand – stare into

the distance – as if by looking hard enough
I'll find that place where the two sides
of the road merge and unite.

from *Poem*

Silverfish, Moth

◊　◊　◊

One swish of itself and it vanished
into the alley between two books.
There was a twilight city in there,
      leather and paper and dust,
where it had eaten itself a home.

You see it mostly going away,
A virtuoso of departure,
all tail, flickering into absence.
      Its shine is a non-colour,
the blankness of cloud in a window.

At last I had one, the tapering
torso of linked, metallic segments,
the helmet of head with four feelers,
      three more feelers on the tail –
feeling, like fleeing, is its business.

They call it bookworm. Its soil is words.
It is a fish that swims in the dry,
a full-grown caterpillar, a moth
      that flits among the pages,
having no need of wings. Unlike this

plumed moth, its four wings soft as an owl's,
a tired angel I found on my wall
in the splayed pose of proclamation.
      It was tufted all over,
body, legs, wing-stalks, even the horns,

brushes of fibres to catch the air.
The plumage differed, like that of birds,
according to the part it grew on.
  Days later I was finding
white specks lodged in my skin, moth-feathers.

   from *Poetry Review*

CLAUDIA FRIEDRICH

My Disseration No Plagiarisation!

◊ ◊ ◊

For this it needed demand and
there was none.
My me written is no,
and the reject I all emphasis.
It about over years, next
job and as young in
painstakingly originated,
and contains undoubtedly.
And over single of this
am I unhappiest.
Was however no time cheated
or the authorship identified.
Should someone hereby or
footnotes and pages, hurt,
so I genuinely sorry.
The extensive and evaluation mistakes
the university responsible.
I will actively help, to what extent
can academic and emphasise
a misconduct found.
And I happily until result
of this temporarily I temporarily
renounce holding the,
but until then.
I would hold again.
I me no standard use,
I them used others.
Every following about this
I will now on via
the Bayreuth direct.
People in country expect,
I me the challenging as

Minister of Defence
full energy, and that I too.
Stand before historic
Bundeswehrreform,
I have responsibility for soldiers in,
like a today,
once more, bitterly.

from *Kaffeeklatsch*

A Room at the Grand Hotel des Roches Noires, 1971

◊ ◊ ◊

Madame likes to air the double she takes for eight weeks
on the sea-facing east wing.

She has written twelve postcards to Brussels in a month.

Her tone – *La mer est jolie* – is light and blasé though
she counts six instances of the word
                                    ténèbres.

Arthritis has touched her best hand. Outside the sea
glances her way with distance

where once everything in the world was a man
asking her to dance.

On one shelf in ribbons, her empty hatbox deepens

into deeper hatboxes that collapse slowly
                            into the green pinochle halls
                            of the pinochle men she knew.

Madame dreams in the window chair

and sees her postcards
from the Roches Noires
fly lightly down

                            over the swathe of sea
                            from the undercarriage
                            of an albatross.

The ocean bird migrating   but so everything seems
at this point

> the cad with a tall white grin
> throwing double sixes at midnight
> fresh oysters with their slight cologne
> in the backseats of young France

The concierge is calling her
—*Madame. Madame?*

An old albatross the scuffed white of lobby magazines.

An old albatross, but content as she wanders off the edge
of the continent.

from the *London Review of Books*

DAVID HARSENT

Fire: end-scenes and outtakes

◊   ◊   ◊

Ils sont dans l'air, / Les ossements.
                    GUILLEVIC

Dry bedrock, the scorch on corn and kale, the first of the last
on dreamtracks and flyways, a pilgrim-line stretching back
to jots on a long horizon, mile on mile through a pall of simple dust.

It will come to fire, so they say, despite the roar and roll
as continents calve from the ice-fields, as rain-forests fall,
as the sea first takes the lowland then takes the rest,
fire nonetheless, fire on the skim of the sea, fire at the core.

My children's children will stand outside the law, to wreck
and break, to witness, to set fires, to fall on the weak.

★

When women howl in the streets, when husbands stand at their doors
with kitchen knives and baseball bats, when children stare down
through window-bars, when asylums empty in a shower of glass,
when Threadneedle Street is a DMZ, when men of God go on all
        fours,
when the shadow of a hand imprints as stain,
when the Politburo signs off, when fear is farce, when whores
walk out in holy blue . . . there's the butt-end of prophecy for sure.

When the peregrine catches the updraught, a sudden flame
kindling along its pinions; when it tips and stoops through the blaze.

★

City backstreets in nailhead rain, transports at every junction,
engines idling. The roundup lasted all night. They could take:
Clothing, one parcel. Food, a half-ration. Personal items, none.
Houses burned in the rain. The charred wood seemed to soften
then fall in on itself. Glass breaking everywhere.

They sang through the downpour. One woman had with her a book
that mapped the set of the stars, but nothing was given there
of how fast they were lost, or how often
they would stop to offload the dead in that breaking dawn.

A scatter from the tailgate: letters and lists thrown down.
You might guess their song wouldn't carry in such dull air.

★

Notebook: *(Dieter Klein)* –
. . . the plan: to go always at daybreak;
wake them and load them; ship them out . . . Their names
were of no account. Did they sleepwalk down the street?

★

The trucks clattered on. The wastefulness of prayer
was a hard lesson. Her book was 'Starcraft'; on the flyleaf, natal charts
for her children which read wrong
in all houses – no dark hand evident – and made of her a liar.
She held them close, her litany timed to the tap and tap of their hearts.

★

A walled city, where the godless went through; this same square
piled high with trophies: which might mean treasure
might mean body-parts; and children spiked on the ramparts, so we're
        told.

As they rode down the Street of Locks and out to that red-rimmed, bare
landscape, the firestorm crowned above the rooftops, gold
leaf lifting and crusting, the great domes stove-in, everything rare
brought back to clinker and smudge . . . a goat's head in the smoke.

It burned for days: percussion of flame on the threshold, on the stair.
The priests heard it first in their sleep and died as they woke.

★

NOTEBOOK: *(Anon)*
. . . and everywhere torn down, defac'd, defil'd
or put to the torch: the sacred image of Christ Pantocrator.

★

When troops deploy at the crossroads, when they line the abyss,
when the glorious dead desert the necropolis,
when some slight smile leaves a scar, when what's guilty is what's to
     hand,
when the merciless doorstep the innocent,
when psychopaths enlist: a means to an end,
when children take to the streets,
when art tends to corruption, when animals turn
from the fire in the forest to face the fire in the cage,
when this fool is that fool's stooge,
when rape is a sweetener, when the unloved prompt the unborn,
when aerial shots reveal the macula
of turned earth, when spirochete and bacillus tumble in gutter-waste,
when money can buy only money, when the infill is hair and teeth,
when the ballast is bones . . . then it's much as you might have
     guessed . . .

★

Dreamwork delivers jump–cuts: dust across the sun,
a killer-wind through the shanty, the long, slow stare
of the dying as they fade, the crackle and flare
of phosphorous, mother and child taken up as one,
the horizon ablaze, just as the fires
rolled in on the settlements, the sound, it was said,
of a train bearing down on the wretched, who left everything, who left
the new dead without pomp or prayer.

★

They lock their doors behind them. They are carrying all they own.
They come, in time, to a place of walls and gates.

———

There's smoke in the sky from fires that can't be seen.
Years later, a bas-relief of this goes up: a shrine,
profiles, fused in grief and fear; each starts
where another pauses for breath, or turns to speak, or crouches down
to filch the pockets of the dead: the way it was. A man
has covered his face with his hat. The stone darkens in rain.
If you look long enough, and hard, a shudder goes up the line.

★

NOTEBOOK: *(Transcript)*
Our arms ached from the work of cutting throats; we seek
redemption, even here, as we kneel in the field of skulls, our prayer
to be unremembered, or numbered among the meek;
that the tally — our working day — be fed to the fire.

★

Water pours in and lies undrinkable. Bodies knock in the drift.
Even so, it will be fire. Floodwaters shift
earthworks and woodland, villages go under, the rumble of mud
brings carrion-eaters to the outskirts, brings them overhead,
and tides under a hard moon, never so bright,
fetch cars and beds and gable-ends, cattle gaffed
by the wire that fenced them. Even so . . . The bed-
time story is fire, the fairy-tale is fire, the promise of light
to a dying man is really a promise of fire. What's left to be said?
A mother calls to her child. The dead call out to the dead.

★

NOTEBOOK: *Though rivers unload, though the seas grow higher,*
though standing rain is a day-long widening wall,
it will be fire, it will be fire, it will be fire . . .

from *Poetry London*

The Oak Coffer

for for my uncle, Alfred Miles
1909–87

◊   ◊   ◊

'they created a desert, and they call it peace'
and that could have been said of Carthage,
though it wasn't. It was much closer to home.
Scattered blocks of stone, and dust, the stumps of houses.
And now left with men who lie, no matter what,
for little reason, vanity or fear,
but who lie, amid smiling cruelty.

'Now how will the little people get out of this one?'

There was a stagnation, the lily pond clogged with weed,
fish deformed, as people drift, as I drift.
Some forms of inertia and indifference

while every Saturday morning you polished
the oak coffer, week after week.
The scent of beeswax in that narrow hall.
The wood polished till you could see your face in it.
A decent man who'd always been told what to do.

It goes so deep, the anger and unspoken stories.
To curse 'the bosses'? That's another story,
and along with all its contradictions.

Your father – ex-soldier and drunk,
at times a gardener at Windsor Castle –
who in hard times put his children in an orphanage.
But you survived in one way, though with
so much missing. 'We manage.'

To gently run your finger along the edge
of the wood as you pass by.
Keep this memory close of dear virtue.

'Say that to me quietly.'

You made a toy fort from scraps of wood,
painted it late on winter evenings
when the child was asleep.
The steady drone of bombers overhead.
The years pass. Beyond the plywood walls,
out in the open, grief woven in our hearts.
Martha Mavroidi sing, we may get through.

from the *London Review of Books*

from *Within Habit*

◊ ◊ ◊

In the space of a few lines | you may find yourself | in the space of a
few lines | roomy enough to dwell in | some cloudy morning – the little
adjustments | falling makes | in the receptacle | from which   the desire
to receive | somatic perfume | of the pressure drops   halfway through |
the sentence | make themselves felt as distinctions from a state | of deep
sleep | landscaping. Working as agents   induces an improper feeling
of flatness | sex flowers strike | so light   it hardly registers as defeat | the
tears or weak areas. To determine   the appropriate pressure | for

movement

to be deterred | partition calls back the candelabra-form espalier called a
palmette verrier | from which falls | at close intervals a   downpour of |
stops. High over | an area of rainforest | makeshift   barricades are erected
| to distinguish the trees | from the wood to form a thick, impenetrable
| paywall | against environs. At the touch of your | music | ash dissolves
harmlessly | as though from a great height | to reveal the shape of | my
own hand holding | my own   hand holding | my own hand back from
| its element. Meliboeus, please, we all make mistakes | the price of |
watching their flight.

from *Magma*

A loop of jade

◊   ◊   ◊

When the television has stayed on too long, the channels ended, and all
the downstairs lights switched off but one, sometimes, rarely, my mother
will begin to talk, without prelude or warning, about her growing up.
Then her words feel pulled up from a dark and unreflective well – willed
and not willed. It isn't that this tacit contract is not tinged by our same
daily fumblings, but when the men are asleep, I think she believes it's
someone else's turn to listen.

Once she spoke of her horror, as a very small child, of the communal
kitchen in their low-rise tenement – half-outdoors in that muggy climate,
it ran across the whole row, a corridor or terrace; this space, aside from
housing a blackened, static wok the size of a Western baby's bath, was also
a latrine. Of squatting barefoot over the cracked tile trench and trying not
to breathe. How her eyes would involuntarily follow to the nearby drain,
as it sprouted – here she giggles, shivers – the glistening bodies

of cockroaches, like obscene sucked sweets. I see them, the colour of rust
or shit, hitching up from the crusted grille on agile legs;

things scuttling from some dank, subterranean chamber of the head.

★

A pendant of milk-green
Jade was meant to bind
Our two young lovers.
So when Zhu was given
To another, older man,
Liang's winged heart
Stopped its fluttering.

★

Another time she tells of being made, in the bucket room, at the place she alway
calls a school, to wash her hair with a green detergent meant for scouring floors,

shaken from a cardboard tube. Unconscious fingers reach towards her scalp. I d
not look for the candied rose petal patches – there as long as I remember – as c
mange or burns, that tell why, before leaving her room, she will so carefully laye
and arrange her lovely black hair.

★

I can never know this place. Its scoop of rice in a cracked grey bowl, its daily thin
ning soup.

Harbour thunder echoes in their sleeping room: outside, the rattling, clanking bi
of boats. She huddles closer to the other girls. On slight brown arms, hairs begin t
lift. The brightest smack of lightning will induce (can this be right?) the bunk's iro
frame, like some kind of celestial tuning fork, to zing with a preternatural hum –

a night-dead television set, its autumn storm. An inch from the wrought bar
buzzing, her child's hand trembles. I feel my own palm magnetize to hers; bu
something holds it back. The metal has a funny smell:

a smoking wok, or caustic soap.

★

They interred him by
The mountain road.
From the casement's
High lattice she wept:
A caged cricket. Soon
Came the wedding day
Of Zhu Yingtai, mocking

★

She tells these and other stories with a pause-pocked, melodic, oddly datable hesi
tancy. What I mean by this is, whenever I hear it, that halting intonation takes m
back unfailingly to the years when we first moved here. I needed some time t
work out why. In those days, in her early forties, in a new country, she spoke mor
slowly than now, and with a subtle, near-constant nasal hum, more of a *nnnnnn*
– so natural to Cantonese –

but which filled the gaps between her otherwise fluent English like the Thereminy strings in a Mandarin film score. As she chatted with the mothers of new friends, tentatively-made and dropped-off to play, it seemed to me that every minute or so – I could feel it building – she would stick mid-note: raised hand stilled, chin tilted in the doorway, a wound-down marionette I willed and willed to start up its song again. A tic the local children mocked me for – that *nnnnnnnnnnng* in the playground –

as I tried not to be ashamed.

★

> *What could never be.*
> *But a magic whirlwind*
> *Stuck fast the procession*
> *So they could not pass*
> *Liang's wayside grave.*
> *The draped bride, craning*
> *Stepped from her chair –*

★

Her longest and most empty pause, I've learned, comes before the word *mother*.

As in, *My – mother, she could speak Shanghainese.* This, one of her startling and thus faintly comical non-sequiturs, arrived while scraping off dinnerplates a few months after a trip of mine to Shanghai. It's as though she's been conducting the conversation in her head for some time and suddenly decides, disconcertingly, to include you. Or, one Christmas, tucking the cooled mince pies into kitchen paper: *I sometimes think she wasn't very – reliable, my –*

mother. What she told me, I don't know how much – I can believe.

In her mouth that noun worried at me. For I would never naturally use it myself – *mother* – except at an immigration office, perhaps, to total strangers, or in the boundaries of a poem, where people are always archetypes, more or less. She places it in the room's still air with a kind of resolve, and yet a sense it's not quite right – a mistranslation –

like watching her wade, one dredged step at a time, out into a wide grey strait – myself a waving spot, unseen, on the furthest shore.

★

> *With a clap of thunder*
> *The tomb cracked open,*
> *Yawned to a ravine.*
> *And Zhu, her silk soles*
> *Balanced a moment*
> *On the earth's red lip,*
> *Hurled herself in.*

★

There was　　　　a man　　　　in a nearby district.
When I was　　young and my　　　　mother short
of money there　　was a while　　　　a lot of
times actually　　when I was　　　　sent to live
with other people.　　That man was　　　　one of
those people.　　Looking back　　　　it was better
than the　　　　school on Macau.　　I learned more
at his house. There　　　　were other children
other　　girls there too.　　　　At night
he would teach us　　the old stories　　　　all
singing together.　　People　　they used to
talk　　about him.　　These weren't just
nursery　rhymes though　　I had never heard
those before either.　　I mean　　the classical
legends and tales.　　He had a　　bad
reputation.　　The legends　　like Shakespeare
had a lot of girls　　who　　dress up as boys
so they will be allowed　　to go to school
or to war.　My　　mother heard about it
had me　　sent back to her.　　When I was old
enough I had to go to the　　school instead.
There was one　　'The Butterfly Lovers'. It
was a poem　　and also a song.　　I used to
be able to sing it all. He was　　kind to me.
I don't think I ever　　taught you　　that one.

——

Some god was watching
Our lovers' one grave –
Breathed down a breeze
Into their broken husks:
Their souls, now two
Butterflies, flicker away,
Never to be parted again.

★

It thuds into my chest, this pendent
ring of milky jade –
I wear it strung on an old watch chain –

meant for a baby's bracelet. Into its
smooth circlet
I can – just – fit a quincunx of five

fingertips. Cool on my palm it rests –
the sinople eye
on a butterfly's wing. When I was born

she took it across to Wong Tai Sin,
my mother's mother,
to have it blessed. I saw that place –

its joss-stick incensed mist, the fortune-
casting herd,
their fluttering, tree-tied pleas – only later

as a tourist. As for the jade, I never wore
or even saw it
then. The logic runs like this: if baby

falls, the loop of stone – a sacrifice –
will shatter
in her place. Painfully knelt on the altar

step, did the old woman shake out a sheaf
of red-tipped
sticks, and pick one, to entreat my fate?

And if I break it now – will I be saved?

from *Poetry London*

Bruisewort

◊   ◊   ◊

I can no longer make a daisy chain that is the sum of its parts.
The joins lack mindlessness. The split stems are DNA strands:
backbones of sugars and phosphates linked by invisible ester bonds
like children's crossed palms, swallowing the weekly good intentions in
        white
unleavened disks that are neither sugar nor phosphates. They taste of
        hands.

To discover the atom is a start – to know what it means; its particle trinity
that has oceans cleaving to the tilted earth resisting the moon's recurrent
        invite;
miraculous photosynthesis, which is bodiless, yet we grope about for its
        photon torso.
If I reassess the sum of its parts, does the daisy chain become divinity,
since the electron and its positron hold the pattern of our future
        infinitesimally?

This is more modellable than we would like to concede. Its Latin name,
        a propos,
means pretty-everlasting. You could say interminable-beauty, but that is
        evaluative,
not quantitative; besides, they were once called bruisewort. Names are
        generally
variable. A daisy chain is not, as the eye would allow, a succession of
        weeds:

each one is a composite flower, whose petals are not just correlative,
but are individual flowers. Even the yellow centres comprise microscopic
        flowers.
They are an army of atoms; of would-be flowers working together to
        spread the seeds
of their existence. If their astral particles are the emblems of probability,

should we swallow the astringent petals weekly and see what follows?

Ø to know how anti-particles balance the pseudanthium with all its
    quarks!
With a fast enough machine, we could decode the daisy chain in calculus,
    Objective-C,
transcendental equations. Would the parts of its sum be atoms or litanies?

from *Poetry Proper*

No Fish Are We Now

◊ ◊ ◊

A fortnight adrift, the crew spot a mermaid
and try to harpoon it. Thus we lose our harpoons.

The masts felled by round shot, I send crew to hoist them.
The splintered trunks bloody us. Thus we lose blood.

Cracked lips and calenture: the midday sun makes us
squabble, spill water. Thus we lose water.

The disguised girl midshipman, clutching her stomach,
makes off with the rowboat. Thus we lose the rowboat.

We slice into bandages, and later, into winding sheets,
the crumpled sails. Thus we lose our sails.

The cook, without a task, goes mad and we must
put a knife through his heart. Thus we lose heart.

Brown, nude and stumbling; in the heat of death
we strip rank, pips, order. Thus we lose order.

The final few cudgel the brash navigator, croaking
songs of their homeland. Thus we lose land.

Even I cup the seawater, knowing its curse
and wrestle myself. Thus I lose myself.

The mermaid returns, as I curl, undisturbed,
on the deck. In time she is lost to the waves.

from *The New Statesman*

ALAN JENKINS

Deptford

◇ ◇ ◇

At closing time:
Conspirators, old salts
Who knew the ropes!
I steered my leaky tub
Past Davy Jones's Vaults
To the Mermaid Club –
Grapplings, gropes,
A rising tide of slime . . .

Looming through the fog
Came this sea–dog
With a burnt-out stare,
Sweat-stained linen suit;
Chewing on a wet cheroot,
He necked a grog ration
(Though it was scotch)
To stoke his passion:

Welcome aboard, son,
He roared, *It's your watch! –*
Your grandfather, big man
In Malaya: you've seen him
Billow down the quayside,
Shouldering aside
Salt air, come to scan
The far horizon

For the prize
All true-born Englishmen
Had their eyes on;
The whiff of rubber,
Money, and a stiff

Pink gin — old-school,
Born to rule; what if
You'd been him?

Miles upriver,
The bastard Tories
Sail on forever;
Propped on pillows
When you were small,
You read their stories,
The Wind in the Willows
To The Cruel Sea . . . *Poetry?*

A fucking revolution
's what this place needs.
While England bleeds,
Good Queen Bess
Pisses on us all.
Her kingdom for a horse —
Get out, for Christ's sake!
Take a different course!

He stumped off, drunk,
Dragging one sea-leg,
Marlow of the Surrey Docks
Or the Seamen's Mission
In the Old Kent Road . . .
Beneath my bunk, I'd stowed
A walnut tea-keg:
Heirloom, camouflage,

It kept my powder dry
While I pursued their craft —
Now as I cast off aft
I heard a cough, a croak
From that old soak
Sprawled in the stern —
It was myself, come back
To scold me; *Our royal ship,*

He rasped, *is run to rack*
That was so stout and trim
And some are put unto their shifts

Either to sink or swim.
I saw a fusewire snake
Towards a gilded barge;
Saw a match fizz and burn –
It was blown sky-high!

from *New Walk*

Bringing Down the Stars

◊ ◊ ◊

As a mouse sniffs for cheese, so I, reading novels,
am sniffing out scintillas. Sometimes they are few

but enough to keep me going; at other times, rare
and completely enchanting, whole pages, paragraphs,

bring starlight down to earth. Over these I dither,
snuffle back and forth, inhale, raise my nose to weather,

glue it down to sniff the spark, to take the hit again.
I am on the trail of genius whose albedo is nothing short

of fallen snow's, desert sand's, who brings me the sky
'dove-gray with stars', 'the diamond lights of Yalta'.

Under such diffused reflectivity through time and space,
what difference does it make if here we are at Seven Dials

where the sundial pillar boasts only six blue clock dials
since it counts itself as the seventh or on Upper Street

where blue Christmas lights twine round London planes,
each trunk a princely stag, each branch a starry antler?

from *The Rialto*

The Other Family

◊　◊　◊

The boy blows bubbles
at the camera in a garden
of yellow roses,
then the woman blows them,
then the boy.
You tumble up
from a fake fall, your jaw
meeting the boy's fist,
his arms flailing wildly,
you unfurling punches
that don't connect,
don't come close to that,
dancing backwards on your toes
to the kitchen door.
This is years ago,
the woman at the sink
in an orange dress,
hands lost in the suds,
watching the man and boy spar,
the man teaching the boy
how to be a man, the boy
recalling a bubble's
holographic light, or upstairs,
the box room with its
wallpaper of bridges and blue trains
where he woke early to a spot
of sunlight on the skirting board
which made him think
of birds or god until he heard
your key click in the door.
And the woman downstairs
stacking dishes, thinking

of the night she woke in,
moonlight sliced across
the rug, the empty space
beside her, not knowing
where you were.
This is years ago.
The camera has stopped rolling
but we are spinning back,
frame by frame,
the boy, the woman,
you – driving in your car,
driving miles, all night,
with money in your pocket,
coming home
with what you know.

from *Kaffeeklatsch*

LYDIA MACPHERSON

Lithium Lovesong

◊　◊　◊

My element, seamed in stone
and tethered now between helium
and beryllium, a foil balloon pulling
at your moorings, your supple almostness
fingers gravity, kissing air and blackening
with it. As hard to cut as moonlight,
you're pulling me like a tide away
from knife drawers and cliff edges,
safety-netting my amygdala.

Unmaddened and inhibited,
I pop your blisterpacks like bladderwrack,
put on your drugged armour like some new crustacean.
You are the lulling surf in my heartbeat,
the ozone in my metalled mouth,
the wavering in my fingertip: take me
to the smooth sea's bed and tie me down,
wrap me up tight and level me,
let me learn to live a flattened life.

from *Days of Roses*

Modu and Mahu

◊ ◊ ◊

Modu and Mahu will split at the end of the news.
It's rumoured on good authority Modu and Mahu
can't work together
one second longer.

The news is about the savaging of a thousand
at a market, next it's about the English poor
explaining how
they live now.

Then it's about the English rich explaining
gently why. Then it's the tale of a boy
boiled in a war,
then what that's for.

Then it's about a limp and stretchered sweetheart
dug from rubble brightly lit somewhere.
Which goes to prove
her god is love.

Then a word on the multitude under the ruins and then
it's about the House of Pillycock again
in their stately pile
then it's sportsfile

and businessblurt and weatherglance, and then
And Finally it is rumoured in rumour circles
that the comedy duo
Modu'n'Mahu

have split, it's the end of an era for Modu'n'Mahu
fans. – It was sad what happened next, how Modu's
subtle thoughts
on news and sports

spun suddenly round and he bawled in his solo show
Mahu Is A Bit Like That, A Bit Like A Prince
Of Pillycock!
Pilly! Cock!

he sang He Should Die! In That Earthquake They Had! And Mahu
he took to Twitter & Gutter & Splatter to counter
Remember Modu?
You Don't, Do You?

He Matters As Much As Gossip in That Town
They Were Torn To Bits and Ya Don't Remember Them Either!
#mahu
#iloveyou

and someone we won't call anything to protect him
said that was sad and Modu In His Sitcom
and Mahu
In His Film Debut

both separately said to that punter Sad? Sad?
Sad? No! You're Sad! Your Mother's Sad!
but my mother's dead
And Your Mother's Dead

Too! Ha! (Modu) Fuck Her Then!
(Mahu) Oh! No! I Forgot! I Can't! She's *Dead!*
(Modu) Yeah You *Can!*
(Mahu) Are You A *Man?*

it's all in their great reunion gig I just got
from Amazon as I went out, they're long gone now
they were giants
man they were giants.

from *Poetry London*

CHRIS MCCABE

The Duchess of Malfi

◊　◊　◊

*Spoken by the Duchess who has secretly married her steward Antonio and prema-
turely given birth to his child. When the Pope intervenes Antonio flees, followed by
The Duchess, but they are separated as Antonio has to leave for Milan with their
son. Antonio is stabbed under mistaken identity. We are here, Blackfriars, 1614.*

This is The Cut　　　the last act of Drunkenness　　*A
deep pit of darknesse*　　　these actors rule Dramatis
Personae　　just two of us in the cast, Antonio　　a
neon rickshaw at Waterloo　　In this gloomy world
there are bars run by horses　　midníght bookshops
　　　our morals AWOL with dwarves　　To be a
lover in the winter　roots in our nerves　when all soíl is
dead　　A red door in the Thames, the river its hinge
　　letterbox too lean for skulls to fit　　when I lose my
keys, will you let me through　to eternity　I'm
in a red pláy with a real toy sword　　you imagine
my full attention　　　　imagine me wanting
you watching this　　　　who's watching who?
Speculatrix　　　*Now there's a rough-cast phrase to*

your plastique   The door opens a riverbed of dog's
teeth, bónes & trinkets   marriage transgressions for
non-privy punishment   Donne with the niece of a
Lock Keeper   imprisoned 1601   In the turn of Act
II we exchange a ríse for a kiss   this is how fucked
up this is blood & florins across the balances   Only
once did we walk Lambeth in daylíght   our organs
turned to purple felt   Antonio, it was not the grínding
war of domestics   children watched us kiss   our
giddiness raged Vs business lunches   a combústion
with invisible cloaks   This question that grínds the
mind's pumice : why has time this death lease? it hurts
to ask   There are more reasons to watch a Duchesse
than to protect her from suitors   then keep to the

Majesty of wedlock, it keeps the devil in flesh
candies over all sins   with a coat of solace &
friendship   To play Intelligencer to your monster
            a beautiful monster   the devil's gentleman
                there is no difference between silence & lies
                    when you're in the reeds, watching us
            The door will open its own red tíde   to a
heartshaped crab   that thinks sideways is right
            because it's what it does

        from *Poetry London*

CHRISTOPHER MIDDLETON

Go With Isaac Rosenberg

◊ ◊ ◊

Afternoon moves on
air now so warm

Among the thin green
pipes of the bamboo

those twitters come
from the chick sparrows

It is tentative, a touch
of air all over the skin

Bless, the word for it
becomes the thing

Go with Isaac Rosenberg
scavenging on the Somme

'Sometimes I find a bible
in a dead man's clothes

'I tear out pages that I want,
and carry them around with me'.

from *Poetry London*

The Mill

◇ ◇ ◇

Over the road
and twice the size of the house we lived in;
five stories at least; white clapboard;
wide as a barn.

The cat reconnoitred.
I followed the cat
clambering this side or that
of the mounting-block steps
then ducking the sack
that drooped like a sleepy eye
almost to block the door but not
and in.

Darkness. Light.
Shadows that jigged
with bran-dust and wheat-dust
and softened the pulleys, the beams,
the ladder fading away
to discover this attic or that
where the miller must be
ignoring me
on my porridgy floor.

And hushed.
But roaring in fact –
the dry continual biblical thunder
of mill-wheels grinding together.
Surely
the heaviest weight in the world;
furious too
with a fury of infinite patience.

Where was I now? I'd forgotten.
No, no, I remembered.
Looking for something I was
like the cat
looking
here between rows
and rows of comfortable sacks
like soldiers asleep.

Looking for this
perhaps –
this handful of grain in a gush
overflowing my hands
at a rickety funnel
like money but free
and precious, priceless
if only I caught it.

Maybe not this.
Maybe just wanting
the doorway again,
resisting the weight at my back
breathing and grinding,
the weight and the dark,
and staring not inside but out
the way I came in.

Was that really my home there
over the road?

That acacia tree by the gate
with its scribble of yellow?

Those snapdragons snapping?

My mother afloat
in a window pane
like a bubble frozen in water?

Surely, again,
but surely, surely not mine.
Besides,
I had turned into dust.
White hands, white clothes, white hair.
And next thing would float away
through white air.

from the *Times Literary Supplement*

ANDRÉ NAFFIS-SAHELY

Through the Rockies

for David Shook

◇　◇　◇

It's my third sleepless dawn on the Zephyr
and I'm in Iowa. Outside my window,
a gopher tunnels out of its purgatory
and wobbles across the sugary snow.

Across the aisle, I watch Tanika crush
grains as pink as the sky, then take
a quick hit on her pipe. She's on the run . . .
Her six kids are somewhere in Indiana;

the last time she spoke to her mother,
the old woman shouted: 'No good
comes of breeding with niggers and spics',
meaning the fathers of Tanika's children.

'I wish I was in the *Wizard of Oz*',
Tanika mumbled as we sliced
through this American vastness.
Sometimes no-place is better than home.

Before long, the passion for sharing
spills into the air, like measles at school,
and everyone's mouths start to thaw.
The smile on the travelling salesman (a Nation

of Islam 5%er) depicts the weird joy we feel
when we survive one too many disasters.
The scars on his chest hug his green gang tattoos:
a lesson twice learned and thus never forgotten.

Everyone here has one foot in life and the other
in the future, or the past. Usually the past . . .
Jane, who looks and sounds like Jessica Lange,
reminisces about her time in the circus:

'It was the 70s, I was living in England,
and you really needed a union card
to get any work as an actress,'
so she spent five gruelling months

touring the continent on an elephant.
Her raw tongue licked the edge
of her jagged teeth: 'The dwarves
were the worst: *mean*, horny things . . .

one night, two of them tried to rape me,
but the bearded lady, my friend,
gave them a hiding they'll never forget!'
At Reno, Jane and the vets in their blue caps,

begin their week of blackjack and slots.
We slow down before Colorado
and during a stop munch our way
through Jane's special brownies;

Lenny, the conductor, plucks on his steel guitar
and yells, '*yo-delay, yo-delay, all aboard!*'
Later, he hands me the day's newspaper:
Russia's invaded the Crimea, again.

If history occurs first as tragedy, then as farce,
then what shall we call this third act
we're trying so hard to survive in?
That evening, as we drew near to Chicago,

the passengers turned to face the horizon in unison,
and I watched a burst of dew crystallize
in the crisp, purple air, and each
molecule grow till it shone like a diamond.

'How pretty . . .', I'd thought, eyeing the burst
fade fast in the distance; sadly
all it meant, as Lenny later told me,
was that someone had just flushed the toilet.

from *Areté*

Summer Solstice, Cumbria

◊　◊　◊

The cranesbill is electric blue in this half-light's super-glow.
The sun has set the light into the ground –
it's no wonder men buried themselves into it
for coal, or for the other side of the sky.

The wet smell of summer is too simple to speak of,
lost somewhere in the undergrowth
with the language of children
and the directions etched inside the mouths of caves.

Still, twilight shoves into seeing
a world behind a sheet of water
or through the eye of a rook.
I rest the shovel against the coal-shed door.

Fennel mixes with the smell of smoke
from the chimney charged with keeping
the sandstone, darkening, dry. The colour of
rust, iron ore. Jacob's-ladder, polemonium caeruleum.

A helix of ivy followed up the wall turns
from dark to neon green.
For a moment, I see the world's weightless ease,
the dream of a woodwose, or a will-o'-the-wyke.

The moment is not enough.
The shovel hews a grike into the coal.
The sky is still not quite slate,
the cranesbill sings, the poppy is deep, dark red.

I am sorry that time moves too quickly for us.
Even now, the sky is pushing for rain
and the damp draws it, the way water sticks,
thicker than the petal coming to rest on the grass.

from *Kaffeeklatsch*

The Chain

◊　◊　◊

Why do I keep thinking about that chain?
I didn't dream it up, I wasn't born
when Moshe Scheiner made it. But yes
if I'd had the skill . . . Torn out of my life
I guess if I found a broom-handle
broken from its head, I'd recognise
something I could turn, with a knife,
to linked medallions. I'd start picturing a cartouche –
no, four or five – between a run of loops.
When does chain connect and when does it spell
prison, manacle, a cry for help, regalia of office?
I'd be, at least, a witness.

Casting chains for the ships of Solomon.

On the first lunette, where the handle snapped
from the worn-out bristles, I'd show us saying goodbye.
Though that was not the word they used –
they spoke French or maybe Polish, and the baby
didn't speak at all. I'd carve myself, a father with his son:
he's hugging my knees while I dandle the little one.
That's where I'd begin, scraping where sap
once rose in a pine-wood heart, aiming not for the under-
image of intaglio but for raised relief: an upper layer,
an outline to tell the world what happened here.
A sequence of, as it were, wood-gems in umber.
Engraved and polished like cameos in carnelian.

Wreaths of chain to ornament the temple.

For the links, I'd try out diagrams in the dust.
Sketching, half-remembering different kinds
of tensile loop – jump ring, pig-holder,
torus, daisy, curb – till I hit on a design like a safety-pin
without the springing free. Copying what swivels do
with studs to prevent tangle, I'd mimic the effect
of a metalworker pulling wire through smaller
and smaller dies, then winding it round a mandrel.
I'd imagine him, my ghost-glass alter ego,
keeping pace with me through the night
in the tiny brilliance of one candle. Cutting,
bending each link closed, then dripping in the solder.

Why stand far off, O Lord? Why hide Thyself in times of trouble?

On the next cartouche, I'd carve myself
walking away from the perimeter fence
at Beaune-la-Rolande. It's only half-built, but I know
the Madsen guns are lining up behind.
I'm alone, lugging timber into that damnable hut
as to a tomb. To represent, to withdraw in your mind,
is not escape. You can't say I've side-stepped reality.
On the third, I'm pushing a loaded barrow
with an armed guard to supervise. For the fourth, no
people: only the low-roofed bunkers, black inside.
On the last, wives and children wave goodbye
to men boarding a train. One day, that will be me.

Shall Thy wonders be known in the dark?

I'd keep the penknife hidden. Brushing ice
from the inner window-pane on winter nights
I'd carve the end into the bearded head
of a patriarch or rabbi. Each of his hairs
takes weeks. Like prayers at Rosh Hashanah
I'm trying to transform sin into grace. A snail
can't crawl on the straight razor and live.
You'd laugh to see the stages, how odd it looked
half-done: a chain sliding out of a stick, a grey pole
alchemising halfway down to honey rings
like dunged straw into gold. And the new work sweet
as a book you treasure but haven't yet cut the pages.

I cry in the day but Thou hearest not, and in the night season.

I'd work along the spindle never knowing
if the links are really there. I'm lost in the river.
Strong bulls of Bashan have encircled me.
Gouging a negative, searching for air
within one wooden oval to begin the next
inside, so they'll shift against each other,
sets me free. But outside or in, still the old question –
is this discovery or true making? Are the forms
of shaping mine? *I will wake the dawn.*
I will toss my sandal on Edom. Blur your eyes
and it's the paper chain my children made
to decorate the hearth. *Will You be angry for ever?*

from *Poetry London*

Girl to Snake

◊   ◊   ◊

We're not supposed to parley, Ropey Joe.
I'm meant to close my eyes and shut the door.
But you're a slender fellow, Ropey Joe,
                thin enough
to slip beneath the door and spill your wicked do-si-do
     in curlicues and hoops across the floor.
I'll be here. And I'm all ears –
there are things I want to know.

   Oh tell me tell me tell me
   about absinthe and yahtze,
   and sugarskulls and ginger, and dynamite and hearsay,
   and all the girls and boys who lost their way
   and the places in the woods we're not to go
   and all the games we're not allowed to play –
   there are so many things to know.

My mother's got the supper on the go.
My father will be sagging in his chair.
But you're a speedy fellow, Ropey Joe,
             quick enough
to slide behind his back, a wicked line of dominoes
      zipping through the hall and up the stairs.
Come on, pal. I'm ready now –
There are things I want to know.

   Oh tell me tell me tell me
   about lightning and furies
   and ligatures and diamonds, and zipwires and gooseberries
   and all the girls and boys who went astray
   and all the ones who never got to go
   and all the words we're not supposed to say –

there are so many things to know.

They told me you were trouble, Ropey Joe.
You've always got to tip the applecart.
But you're a subtle fellow, Ropey Joe,
         suave enough
to worm your way inside and pin your wicked mistletoe
   above the crooked lintel to my heart.
Come on then, shimmy in –
there are things I want to know.

   Oh tell me tell me tell me
   about hellhounds and rubies
   and pretty boys and bad girls, and runaways and lost boys
   and all the things that made my mother cry
   and all the things he said to make her stay
   and all the things we're not allowed to say –
   there are so many things to know.

from *Poems In Which*

Caliban Life

◊   ◊   ◊

Here on the island things are fertile and grey.
Sometimes he makes strange lights.
The girl loves him, the spirit is tired

that lives with him in the mansion.
Sometimes we imagine laughing, biting at the girl's
breast – out here, living the Caliban life.

★

Out here in the wilderness
he can reach us at any time
sending the spirit to sting us with blows.

Will you never learn? he says, and You will never
learn. He knows the lesson is well
taught, forcing music out of nowhere.

★

Sometimes we imagine a marriage
between us and the girl, a ceremony
all serious and beautiful, with a bouquet

of things found on the beach given
as a sign, then our heavy hands, then
no escape, out here, making you live the Caliban life.

from *Kaffeeklatsch*

CAROL RUMENS

Easter Snow

◊ ◊ ◊

'There was a man of double deed
Sowed his garden full of seed . . .'
ANON.

'And so I've found my native country . . .'
ATTILA JÓZSEF

There was a man of double deed
Sowed his garden full of snow,
Lit a stove he could not feed,
Sired a child he could not grow,
Who fashioned birds from wooden blocks,
And when their wings fused flight to dark,
And when the dark swept through the locks,
Fetched a book and made an ark.
But who could sail so deep a ship,
Or marry beast to bolting beast,
Dance as he would his flimsy whip
Over the backs of the deceased?

Poets must tell the truth, you said:
The poor must, too, although they lie.
We listen at your iron bed,
Under the tunnel of the sky,
And ask you softly what you need –
Blue roller-skates? A football team?
But you are far and far indeed.
And all the stumbling magi bring
Is the smoke-haze of a dream,
A floating girl, a greasy bear,
A courtyard echo-echoing

The snowy wing-beats of your heart
Towards the deficit of air
Predicted in your natal chart.

from *The Rialto*

Ethiopia Shall Stretch Forth Her Hands

The Seven Commandments of Joe Louis

◇ ◇ ◇

Joe Louis, mid-clinch,
is lifting his opponent –
the six-foot-six 'Ambling Alp', Primo Carnera –
into the air.
In The Hague
Italian and Ethiopian officials
have come to the end of their first day
of arbitration talks.
Here, in the Yankee Stadium,
Carnera will sink to his knees
'slowly, like a great chimney that had been dynamited'.

For breakfast this morning, Carnera consumed
a quart of orange juice, two quarts of milk,
nineteen pieces of toast, fourteen eggs,
a loaf of bread and half a pound of Virginia ham.
If he took the *Washington Post*
he will have seen a cartoon showing himself and Louis in
the ring.
The illustrated Louis cast a dreadlocked shadow;
his shadow wore a crown.

Louis will start throwing bombs in the sixth round
and knock the Italian down twice
before a right-left combination
ends the fight.
Louis will touch a glove to Carnera's lower back
after the bell, and return to his corner
without celebration.

Louis has been given seven commandments
by his new manager to ensure he progresses
towards a title shot unhampered
by comparisons to Jack Johnson.
He is never to have his picture taken with a white woman.
He is never to go to a nightclub alone.
There will be no soft fights.
There will be no fixed fights.
He will never gloat over a fallen opponent.
He will keep a 'dead pan' in front of the cameras.
He will live and fight clean.

In 1964, Martin Luther King, Jr. will write
'More than twenty-five years ago, one of the southern states
adopted a new method of capital punishment.
Poison gas supplanted the gallows.
In its earliest stages, a microphone was placed inside
the sealed death chamber so that scientific observers
might hear the words of the dying prisoner.
The first victim was a young Negro.
As the pellet dropped into the container,
and the gas curled upward,
through the microphone came these words:
"Save me, Joe Louis. Save me, Joe Louis. Save me, Joe Louis . . ."'

from *Poetry London*

Pilgrimage

for Sam

◊   ◊   ◊

How you loved Jesus –
found him everywhere
even the rank queer bars of Vauxhall.

You would lead his drug-scorched body to a cubicle,
lift his stone-white vest,
kiss his side

injured with the tattooed names of boys
and once
a skin-coloured dove

carrying a twig in its skin-coloured beak –
searching for land
across a sun-tanned midriff.

from *Magma*

Prize-Giving

◊ ◊ ◊

Prize-Giving

The poet P. resents having to travel with me to Italy for the ceremony. He is a full-time professional while I have only just published my first collection. In the airport lounge, he takes out his laptop, puts his headphones on and stares at the screen while I drink my coffee. He only comes to life when one of his female students appears from nowhere. Tearing off the headphones, he picks her up and twirls her around. She is half his age, the same age as my daughter, who yesterday while we were out walking in a nature reserve approached a stag with enormous horns. The stag did not move away, but stared at her with friendly curiosity. It was only when I came near him that he turned and fled.

Youth

Three beautiful Italian sisters lived next door. They were triplets, and all three were in love with me. Everyone said how lucky I was, but when their father demanded I make a proposal of marriage, I didn't know who to choose. For even when I made love to one of them, even when I held her gaze and our bodies trembled together, I never knew which of the three I was with.

Poet's Pipe

In an old tobacconist's shop, I stumbled across a curved clay pipe, like the one smoked by the Italian poet, Cesare Pavese. I couldn't resist buying it. My Italian friends, who were all left-wingers and admirers of Pavese, were impressed when I took the pipe out of my jacket pocket, lit it, and puffed away as if I'd been smoking a pipe all my life.

The next day I was with my friends in a packed car driving down Via Roma in Turin. At the corner of a square we stopped outside a bar frequented by neo-fascists. My friends asked me to light my pipe. That would impress the fascists. They would realise that the lefties had a long-haired Englishman on their side.

I couldn't find my matches. However, as I puffed on the pipe and pretended to smoke it, a glow appeared. Somehow an ember had stayed alight from before.

One of my friends jumped out of the car and went into the bar. He pointed at me smoking my clay pipe. Soon the fascists and lefties were all pointing at me, and they were all laughing together.

City

I lived in Milan. I hadn't had sex for ages, yet one morning I noticed a rash of warts on my penis. I cycled as fast as I could to a doctor's surgery near the city centre. He told me it was nothing to worry about and gave me some cream in a tube with no label. When I came out, I saw a group of gypsy children clustered around my bike on the other side of the street. As I got closer, I realised it was a different bike. Mine had disappeared. 'Someone has stolen it,' I said. One boy raised a large spanner in the air, ready to hit me if I came any nearer. I walked away, thinking that if only I knew how to tell someone my story, I wouldn't feel so lonely.

Town Centre

A thin youth with tousled hair and a wispy beard was walking from car to car stuck in the traffic. He tapped on each window and held out his hand for money. One driver, perhaps to show off in front of the woman next to him, jumped out of his car. Shouting and shaking his fist, he ran after the beggar all the way up the crowded high street. I thought he would catch him, but the beggar, turning a corner, ducked unseen into an Italian restaurant. I found him sitting at a table there, looking at a menu. The tablecloth was piled high with coins he'd taken from his pockets. He invited me to join him.

Needs

I rented a room in an old house owned by an Italian family. They treated me like one of their own. Because one of the daughters was blind, none of the local men would consider her. Her father asked me if I would marry her. He gave me some pretty pebbles she had collected.

I put the pebbles into my pocket and took a stroll into town to think the matter over. On a street corner was a blind beggar. He wanted to know what the clinking sound was. I placed one of the pebbles in his palm. Caressing it, he asked if he could have the rest of them. That way, the sound of the pebbles rubbing together at night would keep him company when he slept on the street.

The Philosopher

During the last months of Nietzsche's life, I stayed next to him in his bed. He lay in his nightshirt, propped up on great pillows, gazing into space. I didn't know if he knew I was there or not. Yet sometimes he would turn towards me with his dark tearful eyes.

'It's good, isn't it?' he said.

His sister Elizabeth would bring in tea for us both on a silver tray. 'This is the first time he has spoken in years,' she told me.

I was glad to be of use, but wished I'd known him before when he was writing his last books of philosophy in Turin: *Twilight of the Idols*, *The Anti-Christ*, and *Ecce Homo*.

My wife and daughter were not happy. After Nietzsche died, I found all their voice mails on my mobile. They had been trying to get in touch with me for a long time – without success, since there was no coverage where I was.

from *PN Review*

'Dooms'

for Roy 'Dooms' Sullivan

◇   ◇   ◇

In '42 the first bolt announced itself, cut a strip from his right leg
and left him grappling the mud, smoke rising from the bloody
cauter. The rain touched his face with the brief regret
of someone who has knocked their lover out.

The second hauled him from the window of his truck, razed
his hairline, and split his brow in factions around the flag of bone.
The boiling water thundered at the cliff, the white rocks
and angry foam. The town shunned him after the third,

which was bolder, and found him out at home as he worked
his yard. Down from the dark brocaded sky the white
bird of it alighted on the power line, then came home tame
to Roy's shoulder and detached his ear so delicately he wept.

And it stayed. In '72, now a ranger in Shenandoah National Park
he learnt the taste of petrichor. But his fourth, he swore
found him out indoors and punched the roof to get to him.
After, he was heard to say *I am not a superstitious man.*

Though he tried to outrun it, at Williams Fork
the fifth caught him up and held him, stroked his body,
was the first to stop his heart. It undressed him, sliding off
his left shoe, laces still done up, and burnt away a shirtsleeve.

The sixth was wild and carried off a sod of flesh, charged him
with its own electrics. His blood was a battery, a wild, high note
which kept him up into the night, the hair he'd left stood up on end.
He crackled when he walked. The grass crisped under his tread.

The seventh came upon him as a god. His written notes recall
a prologue in childhood when, with his father in the field a bright fire
struck across his scythe. But this one, being unverified by any doctor,
must be discounted by the record-book, and forgotten.

from the *London Review of Books*

September 1939

◇ ◇ ◇

London seems peaceful
and somehow rather empty.
I think we're going to be okay
I'm feeling almost happy.
I think we should get married
or have some kind of affair.
I think we should have a holiday:
Devon maybe, can't go to Berlin!
I wonder what they're saying
on the Kurfüstendamm? I'm going
to write to Heinrich and say
this war really shouldn't make
the blindest bit of difference.
Oh, what do you think?
I think we should dress down
and make a habit of undressing
a little more often than we do.
Come, let me help you.
I think we should go to the Ritz
and really splash out.
I think we should pretend
we can't sleep because
the nightingales won't leave us
in peace. I think we should sing
There'll always be an England
and just when we've got the hang
of it we should suddenly stop
and look embarrassed.

I think we should bruise our
mouths with damsons.
I think we should listen to jazz

and move our bodies like this.
I think I'll wear that cardigan
which makes me feel slightly odd.
I think we should go to that restaurant
in Dean Street. I think I'm going
to throw my arms around you
and hold you a little more tightly
than I normally hold you
which will cause you to say,
Please stop, you're hurting me!
I think we should listen to the wireless.
I think we should lie for hours
in a field and look at the sky.

from *Ambit*

Endings to Adventure Gamebooks 22

◊　◊　◊

You're murdered at prayer. Your last words
become wet. The whole Forgotten City upturns.
That band of heroes – the ones
who thought they'd be in time – they were wrong.
Now they take you to the murmuring
water's edge. You were imperturbable
but there is such a thing as *too* noble,
Aerith. The light has spiked, the music has swollen.
The boy who lowers you in, who is so sullen –
now, oh now he'll never be your lover.

　　　　　　　　　　　　　　Game Over.

from *The New Statesman*

Red Shoes

◊　◊　◊

I wanted to own you because I couldn't become
the woman I wanted to be, except in ways
that frightened me more than possessing you

would, which is why I made you do the things
I made you do, all the while watching beauty
dance and sway somewhere beyond me, all

the same; and this is always the master's game
when the pupil has the body he so craves.
So art sets teachers dancing with their slaves.

from *The Pickled Body*

GEORGE SZIRTES

Sealed With a Kiss

◇ ◇ ◇

We were always beautiful. always. When we wrote
each other it was our beauty we were committing
to paper, a beauty composed of forgetting.
It was beauty that caught us, that set us afloat
on the great painted sea of our disasters.
It was beauty that moved us against the tide
of dead water, that slowly pushed us aside
and beached us. Here we met the masters
of our fortunes: time, separation, space
with its inevitable music, the lost boys
of the movies, the sweatered girls, the slow
ring of dancers moving to white noise;
the simple sadness of the hand and face,
the loss of the sealed kiss, the long hard blow.

from 3:*AM Magazine*

REBECCA TAMÁS

A Trip With Werner Herzog

◊   ◊   ◊

'Bare night is best. Bare earth is best. Bare, bare.'
WALLACE STEVENS

I say it's enough for one life
and follow him down the long road
to where gravel meets ice,
to where compasses get sick with magnetism
and go nowhere.

Cold from the top of my split skull
to the reach of my toes
I let the air whistle through the gaps in my chest,
the pockets of space in my knees.

Glaciers moan out their fractured weight
and night pulls the colour from the northern sky.

I had lovers, and a bed of my own,
books, an appointments ledger,
a second hand bike.

He had a mountain range folded in his pocket,
amongst the ticket stubs.

When we curl up against our frozen backpacks
he names the stars, the three sailor's knots,
and the bones of a scattered rabbit.

I never want to go home.

from *Kaffeeklatsch*

Inferno: Canto I

◊ ◊ ◊

Halfway through a bad trip
I found myself in this stinking car park,
Underground, miles from Amarillo.

Students in thongs stood there,
Eating junk food from skips,
    flagmen spewing e's,

Their breath of fetid
Myrrh and ratsbane,
    doners

And condemned chicken shin
    rose like
                distemper.

Then I retched on rising ground;
Rabbits without ears, faces eaten away
                by myxomatosis

Crawled towards a bleak lake
        to drink
                of leucotomy.

The stink would revive a
    sparrow, spreadeagled on
    a lectern.

It so horrified my heart
    I shat
        botox.

Here, by the toxic water,
      lay a spotted trout, its glow
      lighting paths for the VC .

And nigh the bins a giant rat,
Seediness oozing from her Flemish pores,
Pushed me backwards, bit by bit

Into Square 5,
        where the wind gnaws
        and sunshine is spent.

By the cashpoint
      a bum asked for a light,
      hoarse from long silence, beaming.

When I saw him gyrate,
His teeth all wasted,
                natch,

His eyes
      long dead
      through speed and booze,

I cried out
        'Take pity,
Whatever you are, man or ghost!'

'Not man, though formerly a man,'
      he says, 'I hale from Providence,
         Rhode Island, a Korean vet.

Once I was a poet, I wrote
        of bean spasms,
        was anthologised in *Fuck You*.'

'You're never Berrigan, that spring
Where all the river of style freezes?'
I ask, awe all over my facials.

'I'm an American
      Primitive,' he says,
'I make up each verse as it comes,

By putting things
                    where they
          have to go.'

'O glory of every poet, have a light,
May my Zippo benefit me now,
And all my stripping of your *Sonnets*.

You see this hairy she-rat
                    that stalks me like a pimp:
Get her   off my back,

                    for every vein and pulse
Throughout my frame she hath
                              made quake.'

'You must needs another way pursue,'
He says, winking while I shade my pin,
'If you wouldst 'scape this beast.

Come, she lets none past her,
Save the VC, if she breathes on you,
                         you're teaching nights.

This way, freshman, come,
If I'm not far wrong we can find
A bar, and talk it over with Ed and Tom.'

I went where he led, across a square
And down some steps,
                         following the crowd.

The SU bar, where we queued
For 30 minutes
To get a watery beer, was packed;

                    Ed and Tom
Sat at a banquette in the corner
Chain-smoking and swapping jokes.

Here we joined them,
                         till closing time,

the beer doing the talking.

'Look,' said Tom, 'if this guy's got funding
And approval from the Dean and whatever,
Why not take him round?'

'Show him the works,' said Ed, 'no holds barred!'
'You mean,' said Berrigan, 'give him

                                  a campus tour,

Like, give him Hell?'
'That's exactly what I mean,' said Ed.
'Let's drink to it!' said Tom,

At which we all raised our glasses,
Unsteadily, clinking them together above
The full ashtray.

'Hell,' pronounced Berrigan gnomically,
'Is other people. Sartre said that.
Hell is Hell. I said that.'

Now people were leaving,
                         we shifted outside,
Into the cold air,

Where we lingered a moment sharing a last
Cigarette, then split,
                  Ed and Tom going to their digs

Leaving me and Ted to breathe the night air.

from the *London Review of Books*

Fosse Way

◊   ◊   ◊

To-day was once Britain.

Acres begin with running north-west.
There were forks and running due north.
Rich wool. Properly a large town.
Unusually quiet.
The sower guides the wheels.
Square words from the charms.

Start out on the line with turns due north.
It bears once more the fosse before
the town through it. Hardly praised.
The land the views a very stone.
Golden sun.

Trees are not luxuriant exactly.
For the country climbing gradually to higher ground
Sometimes a small down.

The villa at the rich weeks in the way nowadays.
Exactly they were practically Britons.

There are not hundreds south-east of the line.
These rivers beyond were mines practically.
Beyond completely followed.

The richer Britons themselves better had been born.
Comes into conquest were many.
The life. Perhaps they were as many
as twenty in some extremely.

Built of timber only once.

Traces of a staircase glass tessellated
painted by means of the heat led
underneath the walls.
The poorest were a good deal more than our own.

Usually cold.

from *Poetry Review*

Thank you for your email

◇ ◇ ◇

Two years ago I was walking up a mountain path
having been told of excellent views from the summit.
The day was clear and hot, the sky wide and cloudless.
There was only the sound of my breath, my boots treading,
and the faint clonking of cowbells back down the track.
What little wind there was on the climb soon dropped
as I reached the summit, as if it had been distracted
or called upon to cover events elsewhere. I drank eagerly,
catching my breath, and then took in the view, which was
as spectacular as I had been told. I could make out a tree,
a shrub, really (though it being so distant in the valley
below I couldn't say how high), silently on fire, the smoke
trailing a vertical black line before dissipating. I watched
the flames consume the whole shrub. No one came to stop it.
No one seemed to be around to see it, and I felt very alone.
From nowhere a great tearing came: a fighter-jet, low
and aggressive, ripped above me and, surprised, I dropped
on one knee and watched it zoom, bellowing overhead.
As it passed I saw a shred of something fall, a rag, spinning.
I shielded my eyes to see, bewildered and pinned watching
the object, the rag, gather its falling weight, its speed, until
it flumped down without a bounce, only ten footsteps
to my right. It was part of a white bird, a gull. No head,
just a wing and a hunk of body. No leg, or tail, just
the wing and the torso: purple and bloodied. A violent
puddle surrounded it, already mixing with the grit.
Ferrous blood wafted and I recoiled feeling suddenly
cold and very high up and the view swam madly: I saw
for a second the flaming tree as I staggered backwards
and became aware that I was sitting, I had fallen, but I felt
as if I was falling and falling still, my mind unable to
connect the events which were real and terrifying because

they were real, only now I think it was not, perhaps,
a mountain, it was not, perhaps, a shrub on fire, and not
a fighter-jet boring its noise through the sky, and I am
certain now, it was not me, or a wing or body of a broken
bird, but the fearful and forgotten things I've lied to myself
about, and to my friends, and to my family.

from *The White Review*

First off,

◊　◊　◊

take note of my bespoke rabbit-folk, pale,
no meat on 'em (a transient enthusiasm),

as they burst from squiggly silos,
nibbling, nibbling, nibbling, Liebling. Nibbling.

Then see how my consort bod escorts me
in its tight suit like a goon.

And look how I leaf so slowly through your
autonomous scent in the labyrinthine

library of your presence.
This world is like edible earth to me:

edible, certainly, but full in the sense of crammed.
Me, I am but a pin. Sharp, slid into it. New.

Or I'm old, a blunt socket that receives existence's
three-pronged plug that sucks my polished electricity.

(I fill myself also, like a dog fills its wallop.)
Me, I'm the national anthem of somewhere shaky.

You, you're as neat as a particle.
I don't particularly mean you to touch me exactly.

from *Poetry London*

Riddle

◊   ◊   ◊

And how does it move?
Its fat, blind feet pound my hands.

What does it show you?
Murky gold; a rage; where the dust falls.

How does it conduct the light?
With shaggy beats of its careless head.

Where does it lay the curses?
In the thin waters; at the fireside; where the veins open.

What does it hold?
A casket of blue filament.

What does it wish for?
To heap its rough tongue across dainty machines.

How does its warmth persist?
Through the acute force of the hammer.

When does it march with a sombre tread?
When both the wells are empty.

Where does it sleep?
On my bed like a thief.

from *The Rialto*

Freeman

◇ ◇ ◇

Be glad for the city's spirit, the pulse
that moves the crowd forward, for lives that cross
and pass and meet again, for every face,
her smile, his frown, his singing on the train,
for synagogue and temple, Arab and African,
hospital, school, gallery, museum,
for bars and shops, bus stops, that ambulance,
for work and plans, and what comes by chance
in the hip hop chaos, the quantum dance,
for the knowledge, when we die, London goes on living
beyond rush hour, streetlights, sirens, clubs closing,
to birdsong, planes, road sweepers, the Tube moving
to the end of each line to return once more,
for the coming and going, for the key, the door.

from *Poetry Review*

Messenger

◊　◊　◊

We found her in the shadow
of the gas drum;
a pleat of otherness
pinched from her dominion.

Maw like a whale,
head slit to gill air,
a dark scythe
at our feet.

We willed her wings to open
her form take shape,
conflate to airy spaces.
A new crescent moon.

We picked the whole contraption up,
brindled, tawny, creamy throat;
she spilled over our hands
into awe.

Her claws were shriven,
her eyes the eyes
of something fallen,
the weight unbearable

so we sent her onwards,
to beat at the heels
of a young god's sandals,
set her away, windward.

from *Poetry Review*

Caravaggio

◇ ◇ ◇

It's the same everywhere, that dead-time place hidden
in the trees, where the earth's been stumbled flat:
trolley-wreck with nettles, the death of a sleeping-bag,
The one-shoe-and-shitpaper midden under a jig of flies.
Aged twelve, bunking-off alone, I'm sheltering there
because the clean Spring afternoon

just went world's-end dark and wet itself.
Though in truth, I might be there anyway:
I'm drawn to these places, already feel I belong
in them. A dark-bearded man comes running;
he's babying something in his arms – a small easel,
a box of paints. Do I mind sharing my shelter?

He's an artist alright – making me laugh, flattering
with adult confidence: see, his wife's in Italy, he's *so*
bored of talking to the radio. His flat's not far.
Fancy coffee? Of course – school hours to kill again,
an artist-friend to kill them with. At his, the question
is do I know Caravaggio? *I think so* [no].

The curtains stay drawn. He talks about Erotic Art,
shows me Egon Schiele, engorged lipsticky vaginas;
shows me Someone Someone's phallus-dreams. Mug
after mug of whiskied coffee cockling me up until
he says *just look what my strange friend left!*, and drops
on my lap, in a slithery heap, real porn; indefinably

foreign-looking men and women, oiled and sausagey,
doing everything. Its foreignness is its newness to me,
its adultness, its reality. He watches my breathing change.
When I stand my head slews, I'm a wonky trolley.

How soon did I know this was coming, and would be
adult — no dare, no comparing-game with another boy?

Too early-on to say what I now want to: *I'm really
sorry, I better go.* He's so close I can smell his
groin-sour beard; the impossible truth is he disgusts me,
and I'm aching with arousal. He has my shoulders
in a kneading grip. *Do I know
I'm like a Caravaggio?*

No-one knows I'm here. Anything could happen, but
so little does, I'm left ashamed by that too, somehow:
passive as a painter's doll I arch against his kitchen wall,
he kneels. There's a coffee-maker. Near the end, he digs
his nails hard in the backs of my buckling knees, as if in hate.
Why will all this leave me so angry? What will I have lost?

Only my Old Holborn and Rizlas, lighter, rolling-machine,
all left behind when he lets me out — half-shutting the door,
barring my exit long enough to say *must you go, really?
You're still shaking!* Kind hand to my face. *I'm not
a scorpion, you know.* Sour-beard kiss. *When you
come back I'll show you how.* And later

I come back. An April evening, lengthening
blue. All dripping peaceably. In a doorway opposite
his place I wait perhaps an hour, well into undeniable
night. Under my army-surplus greatcoat I'm holding
the small cricket-stump I think I want to smash
his head, his mouth, with. But that flat I now know

inside remains unlit, the dark windows secrets.
I watch the door; he doesn't emerge, he doesn't
come back, and I never see him again.

from *Poetry Review*

from *Notes from Dialysis*

◊   ◊   ◊

The Fields Beneath (St Pancras Old Church)

I make my tour
of the garden waiting room
where the tall trees
wander among the corpses.

I might go past
the last resting place
of Sir John Soane
in his stone telephone kiosk,

or the wooden bench
where the Beatles sat
on their 'Mad Day Out'
July 28th, 1968.

The body of J.C. Bach,
'The English Bach',
lies somewhere near here,
lost to the Railway in 1865.

A plaque remembers him
as Queen Charlotte's music tutor,
who collaborated with someone
and died young.

Perhaps Jerry Cruncher got him,
or perhaps he survived
and is strolling with his friend
in the fields beneath.

I drag my feet
through the backsliding seasons
towards a gate in the wall
with its timetable of opening hours.

Good Thanks

They always ask how you are
when you arrive,
but they know already of course.

It's pretty obvious
from the pleading look on your face
and your dialysis tan

that you're a regular here
and it doesn't do
to say you feel terrible.

You're lucky to be alive,
but you don't see it like that.
You think you're being brave.

A joke might have done
to break the ice between you,
but you can't think of one.

You're that woebegone figure
carrying a satchel,
who isn't funny at all.

The Song of the Needles

Needles have the sudden beauty
of a first line.
They're always new and surprising
as they burst from their paper covering.
They sing as they hit the air.

You catch sight of them
out of the corner of your eye,
glinting softly to themselves
as they contemplate their next move.
What they're suggesting is inspired,
but a certain sadness
attends their description
of what is going on.
You don't know whether to look away,
or accept what they're saying.

If you're lucky you'll feel a pop
as one of them enters your fistula
and a cool feeling of recognition
spreads up through your arm.

from *Poetry Review*

I Inspect the Storm

◊　◊　◊

Is that geezer in a suit really a weatherman?
He's dry as a dead tooth and shiny.
The prince rides a boat down the lane.
Grab his pearls of vapour. Ask him
what he does when his bushes rage
and bending firs threaten his roof.

No, don't bother. Clouds have engulfed the earth.
Wind tears branches off trees. Light
has been removed and I'm alone
on a hilltop with flashes of zip and
thunder groaning blue murder. Raindrops
big as cognac glasses shatter on my head.

The weatherman pats me on the back.
Don't worry. That dog galloping towards you,
borne off in the deluge, it's the sensations
that count, sodden homes and floating cars.
Get under this upturned bowl and count.
Be content with my descriptions, my whorls.

A general move and they appoint me president.
That's all for now is what I should say.
Pull down the weathercocks, let gusts
spin their last. They have placed my boat
in the middle of a rising lake. My task,
merely, is to wait for the water to drain.

Big as a whale a wave comes in,
its white fins curling like graffiti on a tomb
spreading out to hold me. The agency shrugs
as windows smash across the esplanade
and the drowned come laughing back
from shore, toothless and tongueless and wild.

from the *London Review of Books*

WILLIAM WOOTTEN

The Harvest

◊ ◊ ◊

One of those rare and yellowed days one gets
In Wittenberg. There's Faustus in his garden,
Its pleasant airs of lingering regrets;
A small wind goes and ruffles up the linden;
From nearby come the pipings of a flute.
This is a place of lost content grown pregnant
With neglect. A great weight of unpicked fruit
Pulls down upon the boughs, and the abundant
Roses are tangled by thick ivy vines.

Faustus has changed. His eyes have fed their hunger,
That once clear face has been filled up with lines.
He calls back to the house: 'Refreshments Wagner!'
Wagner comes, quick as Mephistophiles,
To set a picnic down upon the table:
Ham, salted butter and a firm goats' cheese,
A crusty loaf, which Faustus starts to nibble.

Wagner pours a wine laid down twenty-four
Short years ago. The years have not been wasted,
For they have left the vintage to mature,
Be subtle and complex. As it is tasted,
We dwell upon how Faustus's right hand
Has turned to vellum, its veins, marks and blotches,
An occult language we could understand
If we would study hard.

                    The sunlight catches
The swilling of the wine, the earth-red-brown
Of dried-out blood upon the roll of parchment
Which spills out of his robe. On bending down,
Faustus intones old words of strange enrichment,

Then there is darkening; then the heavy beat
Of wings.

           We focus on a magpie leaving
The house of Dr Faustus then the street,
Its raddled mob caught in their pitchfork-waving,
The fierce tongs brought redhot from the forge,
As iridescent, flickering, exultant
He cheeks the piebald houses, threads a gorge
Of warm red tiles to lord it unrepentant
Over the Castle Church, before which stands
A monk debating with a Danish student
About debt. And, just as the monk's fierce hands
Are flapping to the heavens, the ascendant
Bird trusts the thermals while his greedy eyes
Are captured by the magic of the market's
Array of meats, the glinting vault of flies,
The pots and bottles, balances and trinkets,
The money that's exchanged for salt or spice
Or grain, the costume of a loud and garish
Huxter who whirls three cups, as, in a trice,
All speculative balls and bets will vanish.
A goat is munching flowers from a barrow.
A stern clerk has been drawing up a bond
For a slim burgher who has come to borrow
Gold. Then the magpie climbs on draughts beyond
That rise among the roofs that keep the huddle
Of poor souls, of the healthy and the sick,
The deathbed, shared bed, single bed or cradle
Icon and cross, the charm and candlestick
Until his haughty wings and ours pass over
All Wittenberg.

           The street becomes a track.
Which leaves to wade its way across the river.
On it a laden cart is trundling back
With what must be the first grapes of the season.
Ahead, an orchard, ladders against trees:
Hands gently put each tender pear or damson
Down into baskets, while the windfalls please
The pigs, then long grass and the sleek brown cattle;
The drovers wake a copse; its partridge break.

The magpie's gaze at last begins to settle
Upon long fields of full-eared wheat, to take
Stock of the men and women at late harvest,
The flashes from their sickles, beads of sweat,
And one who sleeps who has chosen to invest
In a large jug of beer. Now, through the wheat,
Another comes to him. Our bird is lost
In want for tiny gleams of rising, falling
Motes from the husk and grain which have been tossed
Up by the labours here; and he is wheeling
In winnowing desires as our long wait
Is done and ready wings are tucked together
To fall at him as surely as man's fate.
We watch him rapt, then leave the change, a feather
Circling, its quill-tip with a crimson drop,
Then pull back for a crane's view of the crop.

from *New Walk*

CONTRIBUTORS' NOTES AND COMMENTS

MIR MAHFUZ ALI was born in Dhaka, Bangladesh. He studied at Essex University. He dances, acts, has worked as a male model and a tandoori chef. He has given reading and performances at Royal Opera House, Covent Garden and other theatres in Britain and beyond. His poems have appeared in *Poetry Review*, *London Magazine*, *Poetry London*, *Ambit*, *PN Review* and *Poetry* (Chicago). Mahfuz was short-listed for the New Writing Ventures Awards 2007 and Picador Poetry prize 2010. He is the winner of Geoffrey Dearmer Prize 2013. *Midnight, Dhaka* is his first full collection, published by Seren in 2014.

He writes, 'Writing "poetry of witness" is not easy. I tried to write them when memory was fresh and emotion was raw. I was too close to them. Even after thousands of dreadful attempts not a single poem came out of me that's half decent. After many frustrating moments and efforts I realized there seems to be no half way.

'I had to wait 33 years to be able to write about atrocities in a detached way. Passage of time helped me seeing things in a different light.

'Only about 2004 I was able to write poems about the time of atrocities and natural disasters and about life-experiences in general. My poem "MIG-21 Raids at Shegontola" is one of them. I usually know what I will write in advance. I'd think about it most of the time. I don't commit into writing until inner force tells me this is the time. Only then I'd have a go at it in a one blast. I wrote this poem in 2012, but I kept refining it until May 2014.

'The incident took place in December 1971, I was in Dhaka at the time, besieged, and Pakistan declared war against India. Indian Air Force raided the key positions in the capital. General Nazi, the Commander-in-Chief of East Pakistan Army, knew he'd be bombed if he remained in the Governor's House. So he went underground and hid in a building at Shegontola. Bomb didn't hit the house where the General was staying, instead the house next door. I don't take sides. I present the case for my readers. It is for them to decide what to feel or not to feel. The poet's job is to represent the case in an aesthetically satisfying way. Aesthetic is important even though it is ugly for the war victims. There's a beauty in ugliness.

'I ignored the historical or journalistic facts and remained truthful only to the emotional ones. For some, in time of war, gun is better looking than tiger.'

RACHAEL ALLEN was born in 1989 in Cornwall and studied English Literature at Goldsmiths College, University of London. She is the online editor for *Granta*, co-editor of poetry anthology series *Clinic* and online journal *Tender*. Her Poetry has appeared in *The Best British Poetry 2013* (Salt), *Poetry London*, *The Sunday Times*, and *The White Review* online. Her reviews and other writing have appeared in *Ambit* and *Dazed and Confused*. A pamphlet of her poems is published with Faber as part of the Faber New Poets scheme.

She writes, 'The teachers I address in this poem will probably not read it, and this is possibly true for most poems written as an apology; the apologised-to will not see their sorrys. The idea of attempting to apologise to someone in a poem then is quite arrogant, as though the writer doesn't care about the apology itself, using it instead as a tool with which to build a poem. It's a sort of *if a tree falls in the woods* conundrum – if an apology poem is written for someone and they never read it, was the apology actually made? When William Carlos Williams writes to his wife in one of the most famous apology poems "This Is Just to Say", he doesn't even use the word sorry to apologise for all the plums he's eaten, he just makes demands of her: "Forgive me". This self-congratulation is made obvious by Kenneth Koch's parody "Variations on a theme by William Carlos Williams", where the list of things apologised for becomes increasingly absurd and, in reality, impossible to forgive someone for: chopping down a house, giving away all the money, breaking someone's leg. But as William Wootten says in his *London Review of Books* review of Koch, although this is a poem addressed to others, "it likes to please itself." Apologies disguise their self-centredness, but are really just an offloading of guilt, accompanied by excuses, gratifying to the apologiser. More often than not they are artificial in their earnestness. Poems do well to accommodate this.'

ROBERT ANTHONY is a writer living in Brooklyn, New York. He has published in a number of journals, including San Francisco's *tight* and Manchester's *Kaffeeklatsch*. He has work upcoming in *Unthology* (UK) and *Edge* (US). Robert is an artist and a musician as well, and has released several albums of experimental and electronic music in the EU and the US.

He writes, 'I watch the sky through the window in the small room where I write, at the top of the row house. When I write, I look for the hidden meaning in the things around me: the room in front of me – visible through the small doorway in front of my writing desk – with its haphazard furniture and signs of a life being lived; or, from outside, the sounds of cars, people on the street, airplanes moving far above me, invisible. And when the curtain is peeled back: the tree outside, the block of houses with the empty gap just across the street. And overhead: the sky.

'I have always been fascinated by the sky, by the clouds which march across it, or coat it grey on rainy or snowy days. I wonder what the clouds get up to, when they disappear off the edge of the world – I feel as if up there, in whatever playground they're playing in, is where I should be, and I long to reach up, just a little way higher, and touch them, to join them as they journey. When I write, I do.'

SIMON ARMITAGE lives in West Yorkshire and is Professor of Poetry at the University of Sheffield. His published work includes his translation of *Sir Gawain and the Green Knight* and most recently *Paper Aeroplane: Selected Poems 1989-2014*. His play *The Last Days of Troy* was performed at Shakespeare's Globe in 2014.

He writes, 'There's something of Goldsmith's *The Deserted Village* about *Emergency* I suppose, at least in terms of subject matter, though in my version the issue is not so much depopulation as dehumanisation. Marsden, where I grew up, underwent economic upheaval in the seventies when the textile industry finally collapsed, and has experienced several more identity crises since then as we've moved from a mechanical to a digital age. Marsden was at the forefront of the Luddite uprisings, and although the poem isn't a call to arms against machines it's interesting to me that the problem has never really gone away. Philosophically I'm wondering what we're like, as a species, without a job or role to occupy our hands and minds. Subconsciously I might also be contrasting the heroic manual professions of my ancestors with the relatively indolent act of writing.

'The fire station, the post office and the petrol station were all visible from the picture window of my parents' house. One by one they've disappeared, along with other amenities and outlets, to the point where the actual business dealings of the village have become invisible, even underground. I found it particularly interesting when a "fake" fire station was built to service the "fake" world of film and TV. Writing about Marsden encouraged the use of local and family words. Out-menders worked from home, freelancers of their day, correcting faults in finished cloth. Greasy perchers worked in the mills, inspecting the cloth as it hung on a perch. The grease is the lanolin in the wool, still present after it had been through the loom. "All manneration" is Yorkshire dialect version of "all manner of". Marsden is ringed by moors, which are often set on fire (illegally) at the end of the summer, producing a sort of three hundred and sixty degree twilight and a post-apocalyptic aftermath of charred grass and hazy smoke. I wrote the poem after hearing Les Murray reading in Perth. The style, I think, is his.'

MICHAEL BAYLEY lives in Cambridge where he lectured in writing poetry at Anglia Ruskin University. Faber and Faber's *Poetry Introduction 7* released a selection of his work in 1990 and *From the Colony Room,* a sequence of poems, was published by Gerard Woodward's Jones Press in 1998.

He writes, '"Estuary" is a found poem lighted upon in Graham Sutherland's *Welsh Sketchbook.* I've not really done much to the text other than edit and reassemble it, my own words merging with the final lines. The original passage reads: "I wish I could give some idea of the exultant strangeness of this place, for strange it certainly is; many people whom I know hate it, and I cannot but admit that it possesses an element of disquiet . . . The whole setting is one of exuberance – of darkness and light – The life-giving sound of the mechanical reaper is heard. Cattle crouch among the gorse. The mind wanders from contemplation of the living cattle to their ghosts. It is no uncommon sight to see a horse's skull or horns of cattle lying bleached on the sand. Neither do we feel that the black-green ribs of half-buried wrecks and the phantom tree-roots, bleached and washed by the waves, exist to emphasise the extraordinary emptiness of the scene." I came across the passage in a notebook of mine dating back to 1979 but didn't think of turning it into a found poem until quite recently. It seemed so entirely a painter's description of landscape, images producing the thoughts. I put it into stepped-verse which not only appeared to loosen the syntax but reproduced the artist's slow meditation on the landscape before him. The form had the bonus of imitating the ebb and flow of the tide.'

FIONA BENSON's pamphlet was published as part of the Faber New Poets series in 2009, and her first full-length collection *Bright Travellers* was published by Cape in May 2014. *Bright Travellers* is shortlisted for the Forward Felix Dennis Prize for first collections. She lives near Exeter with her husband James Meredith and their daughters, Isla and Rose.

She writes, 'Our old house on the outskirts of Exeter backed onto Mincinglake Valley Park, a large stretch of common land that used to be one of the city's landfill sites. The Park climbs up to meadows, and from there to farmland. I started writing "Toboggan Run" during the winter of 2008/9, when unusually for this country we had some hard snow. I looked out of my study window and could see this barely discernible speck whizzing down the white meadows at the top end of the park a couple of miles away. In fact before I recognised the sled, I thought it might be a dog plunging down the slopes, and in early drafts tried to work in this misperception ("not a dog, but a toboggan") but didn't succeed.

'When we were putting *Bright Travellers* together my editor Robin Robertson asked me what this poems was "about"; he'd just given me Anne Carson's *Glass and God* so I could tell him it was in part about being a "whacher", of finding myself often trapped in watching, and frustratingly held back by that. The speaker is not on the toboggan, they are watching it, and it is the lesser experience.

'"Toboggan Run" is also, simply, about how we are losing our colder climates, and losing snow. I spent some of my early years in Denmark, so snow plays a strong part in my childhood memories – the gravelly sound of my father shovelling several feet of snow out of the driveway, or our dog helping my mother pull our own toboggan. Yet these days snow comes rarely and my own daughters will barely know it. So the sadness of the poem comes from both a personal sense of exile and a muddled comprehension that it is all part of one long decline – from our own softening climate to the melting of the polar ice caps and the ruin of our drowning world. Hence liturgy, evensong, requiem.'

EMILY BERRY's debut poetry collection *Dear Boy* (Faber & Faber, 2013) won the Forward Prize for Best First Collection and the Hawthornden Prize. She is a contributor to *The Breakfast Bible* (Bloomsbury, 2013), a compendium of breakfasts. She is currently working towards a PhD in Creative and Critical Writing at the University of East Anglia.

She writes, 'I went to Margate on a grey day one spring meaning to go to the Turner Contemporary gallery but I hadn't checked the opening times and when I got there they were changing exhibitions and it was mostly closed. I ended up sitting in the café and watching the sea for a few hours. That's partly where the poem started. Another time I was staying in a house in Cornwall right next to the beach and you could hear the waves crashing all night which was sometimes comforting and sometimes deeply depressing. Over time different experiences of the sea and other manifestations of water seemed to be good (if obvious) metaphors for what it's like to try and cope with certain states of overwhelming emotion.'

LIZ BERRY was born in the Black Country and now lives in Birmingham. Her debut collection, *Black Country* (Chatto, 2014), was a PBS Recommendation and won the Forward prize for Best First Collection 2014. She is the assistant poetry editor at *Ambit* magazine.

She writes, '"The First Path" is part of a series of poems, *Scenes from The Passion*, inspired by the artist George Shaw's paintings of the Tile Hill estate in Coventry. The paintings are beautiful and eerie, exploring liminal places – bus stops and underpasses, edgelands and woods – unpeopled in the gloaming. They reminded me of my home in the Black Country. I was living away at the time and, like Shaw, trying to find a way to explore the place I'd left behind. Speaking about Tile Hill, Shaw said: "I haunted this place and now it haunts me." I knew that feeling exactly. The paintings were the key I used to let myself back in. "The First Path" was the first of the poems to be written, after a night spent trying to rescue a little staffie bitch who had been abandoned and locked in the allotments in the falling snow. It was near to Easter and her pitifulness and fear as she streaked, bloody-pawed, through the scrubland seemed almost holy.'

RACHAEL BOAST was born in 1975. *Sidereal* (Picador 2011) won the Forward Prize for Best First Collection, and the Seamus Heaney Centre for Poetry Prize for Best First Collection. She is editor of *The Echoing Gallery: Bristol Poets and Art in the City* (Redcliffe Press), and current deputy director of the Bristol Poetry Institute. *Pilgrim's Flower* (Picador 2013) was shortlisted for the Griffin Prize.

She writes, 'The poem was written on 24th December 2012 and is one of several from *Pilgrim's Flower* that celebrate the literary heritage of Bristol. I was spending Christmas alone and needed a subject of study to engage me. Within a few weeks I'd written four poems on Chatterton: "The North Porch", "What You Will" (which contains a reference to Dennis O'Driscoll who died on Christmas Eve, 2012), "Double Life", and "The Charity of Thomas Rowley". I purchased Chatterton's collected poems and was reading a book of essays on the poet, *Thomas Chatterton's Bristol* (Redcliffe Press, 2005).

'One essay in particular caught my attention: "Visionary and Counterfeit" by Alistair Heys, a meditation on the English Gothic with reference to Blake's critique of Wordsworth, to Chatterton's influence on Blake's "Jerusalem", and, by implication, to the "Chattertonian trope of the builder".

'The Chatterton family had been sextons of the parish of Redcliffe for centuries, and the poet had the keys to the church, making use of the room above the north porch for his writing. Rumour has it he also used the building for his early sexual explorations. In this poem I situate Chatterton in his room, working on the Rowley poems. In this act of creative invention, Chatterton also liberates himself from fixed identity and becomes another; a "builder" in the realm of vision endeavouring to uncover the architecture of reality through poetic discourse. In this realm, Chatterton is no forger.

'Form and meaning are confluent in the poem: it fell into one long disorientating sentence resisting closure – itself a kind of "lunacy of ink" – image built on image in a flow too rapid to be influenced by any authorial intentions, not that I'd had any in the first place, trusting in what I'd absorbed from my reading and visits to the church; and, above all, trusting language to supply its own meaning and content. Egoistic intent is generally incompatible with poetry. As John Burnside has said, "the lyrical impulse begins at the point of self-forgetting".'

ALAN BROWNJOHN's last volume was *The Saner Places* (Enitharmon Press, 2011), a selection of poems from fourteen individual books published beginning with *The Railings* in 1961. His next book will be *A Bottle* (2015). He has also published five novels, the last being *Windows on the Moon* in 2009.

He writes, '"Index of First Lines" was conceived as a series of plausible opening lines for poems in different styles by different – imagined and unnamed – poets, all of which would have developed themes of loss and elegiac tribute if continued. It was written in the early autumn of 2012 and appeared in the *Times Literary Supplement* shortly after a companion piece called "Takes" was published there. In that, a number of actual moments in a relationship – the same one hinted as here – are recorded as brief film scenes, in chronological sequence. Occasionally lines assembled in actual indexes of this kind at the back of anthologies will run on in some cases, and – less oddly, since the poems may have been chosen because they illustrate a theme or belong to a period – they will relate to one another. If my lines accidentally did such, I let them. It seemed to me to give unity to ideas and images exchanged in many moments of a friendship developing over a period of time but abruptly cut short in a sudden and unaccountable way.'

COLETTE BRYCE was born in Derry, Northern Ireland. She lived in London for some years before moving to Scotland in 2002, and later to the North of England where she currently works as a freelance writer. Her poetry collections with Picador include *The Full Indian Rope Trick* (2004), *Self-Portrait in the Dark* (2008), and *The Whole & Rain-domed Universe*, shortlisted for this year's Forward Prize. From 2009-13 she was Poetry Editor at *Poetry London*. She received the Cholmondeley Award in 2010.

She writes, 'The Gaeltacht refers to Irish-speaking communities in County Donegal, over the border from Derry where I grew up. As teenagers, we'd be sent there in the summer to stay with families and learn the language. It was tremendous fun. The title refers to one of the laws of the jungle in our area of Derry during the Troubles. British soldiers were often on our streets, on foot patrols or in saracens etc. "Don't speak" connects with a wider theme of suppression in the book from which this poem comes, *The Whole & Rain-domed Universe*.'

John Burnside is a poet, novelist and short story writer. His most recent collection is *All One Breath*. His last, *Black Cat Bone*, won both the Forward and the T.S. Eliot Prizes in 2012, and he is a recent recipient of the Petrarca Prize. He currently lives in Berlin, where he is a DAAD resident writer.

He writes, 'This poem came out of a personal memory of singing in the choir as a child, combined with a reading of Shakespeare's Eighth Sonnet, ("Mark how one string, sweet husband to another, / Strikes each in each by mutual ordering, / Resembling sire and child and happy mother / Who all in one, one pleasing note do sing: / Whose speechless song, being many, seeming one, / Sings this to thee: 'thou single wilt prove none.'"). It is slightly fictionalised, though it remains a personal tribute to and memorial of my old choir teacher, Norman Edmunds, a man of great vim, generosity of spirit and occasional flashes of violent temper, who taught me as much about life as a young teenager can take in. The most important lesson – one we all spend a lifetime getting into our thick heads if we are lucky – was the idea that the Eighth Sonnet expresses: that there is nothing sweeter than voices singing together.'

Dominic Bury grew up in Devon and now lives and works in London. He has been published in magazines including *Poetry Wales*, *Ambit*, *Magma*, *Iota* and won the 2013 *Magma* Poetry Prize. He is currently working towards a first collection.

He writes, 'Many times have I been out walking late at night, in the hollows and slumps of moor that make up the area of North Devon where I grew up. The moors are blanker here, more reticent to give into the light, and fear somehow takes on a different quality. Not the fear that walking round the corner in a dark alleyway can bring on, nor the type that being far out to sea can sometimes foster. It is somehow deeper, gestated, more primordial. This I think is what drives the tabulated narrative sections of the poem. The three "lore" prose sections in between act as a mythic counterpoint to how perhaps, my ancestors, those people who lived hand and nail with the gorse would perhaps have guarded against, and dealt with the feeling described. Sacrifice, ritual, covering yourself with herbs and entrails to mask your own scent. All things that in the 21st century seem a little laughable, but would have been very real to these people. What plays out in the poem is that fear is very much a construct, rather than a learnt experience, and that fear is often worse than what we find in reality. I hope however that in a world which has become increasingly sanitised, there is still enough doubt to wonder, to contemplate the possibility that there remain things on the edge of our sight, that we cannot see, but still feel.'

ANTHONY CALESHU is the author of a novella, two books of poetry and a critical study of the American poet, James Tate. He won the *Boston Review* Poetry Prize in 2010 for the first five of his 'Victor Poems'. Others have since appeared in *Poetry Review*, *Shearsman*, *Salamander*, *Narrative*, and *Web-Conjunctions*. He is Professor of Poetry at Plymouth University.

He writes, '*The Victor Poems* is a book-length serial poem which charts a group of men as they track their old friend, Victor. Friendship, as a theoretical pursuit, is almost as complicated as love, and philosophers from Aristotle to de Montaigne to Emerson to Blanchot have exposed the paradoxes inherent in friendship as something sublime: "We walk alone in the world. Friends such as we desire are dreams and fables," wrote Emerson. And then Emerson rethinks his own argument: "But a sublime hope cheers ever the faithful heart." Friendship poems have a dubious past. They can be sentimental and trite, for sure. But then a poet like Frank O'Hara, with honesty and heart and a deft command of the language, can make it a risk that demands taking. I started writing *The Victor Poems* after a friend mentioned the Arctic and a man by the name of Victor who was mythical for his potential to save the distressed. I wanted to claim Victor as a friend and started writing poems in the hopes of doing so. The Arctic served as a *tabula rasa*, as something which is both attractive and repellant, as something *sublime*. And then there's Roni Horn who writes so sublimely about paths.'

GERALDINE CLARKSON was born in Warwickshire, one of a family of ten. She spent some years in enclosed monastic communities in both England and South America. She has been awarded a Jerwood/Arvon mentorship, the Escalator Prize, and Arts Council sponsorship. Her poems have appeared in magazines including *Poetry Review*, *The Rialto*, *Poetry London*, *Tears in the Fence*, *Fuselit*, and *Shearsman*. She was Selected Poet in *Magma* 58, and won the 2014 Ware Sonnet Prize. Her work is forthcoming in *Furies* (For Books' Sake) and *The Poet's Quest for God* (Eyewear), and she is currently working on a first collection.

She writes, 'Although starting out as "Grace and Control", this poem was always rooted for me in the physical opposition of the two women. When I tried to steer away from the schematic notion of "control', the name "Laura" presented itself. I realised later that that name contains the word "law", which seemed serendipitous as it suggested the fundamental opposition between grace and the law, which resonates for me. I've always loved the concept of "grace" – its suggestion of extravagance and superabundance, unearned, undeserved, always a little more than is reasonable or expected (sometimes a lot) – wanton, excessive.

'This wasn't in my mind as a scheme as I wrote, but was there, perhaps, in the way I was relating to the two women. I usually write quite intuitively but I can see that I was maybe responding to the two sisters as two modes of being – "life-suppressing" (legalistic?) versus "life-affirming" (grace-full?) . . . Is the poem positing an E.M. Forster only connect moment in that mention of incestuous marriage? I don't think so. "Justice" and "Peace" are said to embrace, but I don't think that Laura and Grace are going to gel any time soon . . .'

SOPHIE COLLINS is co-founder and editor of *tender*, an online quarterly promoting work by female-identified writers and artists. Her poems have appeared or are forthcoming in *Poetry*, *Poetry London*, *The White Review*, and elsewhere. Reviews and other writings are published in *Poetry Review* and *Dazed & Confused*. In 2014 she received an Eric Gregory Award and was a poet in residence at the LUMA/Westbau exhibition space in Zürich. She is currently carrying out research on poetry and translation at Queen's University Belfast. sophie-e-collins.tumblr.com

She writes, '"Desk" is a traditional cento made entirely of lines from other people's poems. The lines used here were all found via the Poetry Archive website and the search term "desk". There was an element of constraint involved in the composition process, given that I made sure to use one line from every poem listed in the search results. (Twelve poems, twelve lines.) The archive's recent renovation means that it's no longer possible to easily trace the poems whose lines have been borrowed. As far as I know, the poems are still up there, but the keyword "desk" now gives zero results.'

JOEY CONNOLLY edits *Kaffeeklatsch*, a print-only journal of new poetry and criticism (with a website at manualpoetry.com). He received an Eric Gregory award in 2012, and his first collection is forthcoming from Carcanet early in 2016.

He writes, 'Although the narrator of "Chekhov's Gun" is (I hope) very definitely not me, the rail station, the polkadots, and the first love are all totally bona fide. (Hi Sophie Marsden from y6, if you're out there. Look me up on Facebook.) I reckon it's been five years since this poem's first draft, so I can't remember what the book I was reading on the train was, now, and I'm only ninety percent certain that the quote is accurate. It's conceivable that "Gerhardie" was chosen, in a moment of poetic *mala fides*, for the rhyme, but it might just as well be true. I'm fairly sure "inscrutable" is plagiarised from an incredible poem which I can't quite place at this moment, but it's now more or less at the centre of this poem. According to etymonline.com (the greatest website) the "scrutable" bit is from *scrutari*: "to examine, ransack".

'"Chekhov's Gun" refers to a principle of composition in drama or short-fiction – something like "if you hang a gun above the mantelpiece in the first act, it must be fired in the second". So I guess the poem doesn't do very much apart from gently mess around with the idea that one thing might make another inevitable, with several guns having been hung up somewhere, years before the opening of the action. Although I suppose it also plays its little parts in the interests I enduringly hold and can't help putting into all my poems: the almost-but-not-quite orderly progression; the strange relation of poetic narrators to authority and truthtelling; and the conviction that ostensibly intellectually complex and/or stonily rational language can often appear to mask (and therefore imply) tons of almost-trite, almost-sentimentally sappy and emotional things. And *vice versa*, also – and *vice versa*.'

SIÂN MELANGELL DAFYDD was born in North Wales. She writes in both Welsh and English and often collaborates with dancers, artists and international writers. Her first published novel, *Y Trydydd Peth* (*The Third Thing*; Gomer, 2009) won her the coveted 2009 National Eisteddfod Prose Medal. Her poetry and fiction can be found in many magazines and anthologies, including *Best British Short Stories 2014*. She is the co-editor of *Taliesin* and www.yneuadd.com and teaches Creative Writing at the American University of Paris and so splits her time between North Wales and Paris.

She writes, 'My father found a footprint in the snow. It was a cat's paw but too big to be a cat. It wasn't a fox paw or a badger paw. It really was a cat. Calculating the size of the print, the distance between each paw and its stride, the distance from the fence where the prints stopped, and the metre-high fence itself, this animal must have been over two feet tall and strong. A photograph of the indent in deep snow circulated by e-mail to family members and no answer was found. Somehow, the idea of these roaming, large, yet invisible creatures took hold. I became fascinated by people's accounts of sightings and traces, looked at online maps of where it seems, they might be. It is possible to map the country through sightings of animals, which, according to some, don't exist. The voice of someone who had been "visited" by this presence came to me, a thing unknown even to someone who is intimate with their surrounding landscape.'

JOE DRESNER was born in Sunderland in 1987. After working in an art gallery in London for three years he now teaches English as a foreign language in Sichuan, China. He has had poems published in magazines such as *Poetry Review*, *The Rialto*, *Stand* and *Ambit*. He was also anthologised in *Stop Sharpening Your Knives* (5).

He writes, 'This poem is the first part of a triptych I wrote about three years ago.

'At the time I was, and still am, interested in unusual or antiquated communities. The prohibition against green food towards the end of the poem for instance was a medieval truism. I was reading Ian Mortimer's excellent medieval biographies of Plantagenet Kings, particularly his experimental biography of Henry V, *1415*, which uses a single year to recount the life of the controversial monarch.

'I was also becoming interested in Chinese history and culture. Peter Hessler's excellent book *River Town* provided the detail of the warm brick beds which were used (and I think still are) by the Chinese to warm their houses.

'In the middle of the poem there is a description of repeatedly waking and sleeping. I actually got the idea for this passage from a reading given in a London book shop by Mark Ford. Towards the end of the reading I was zoning out a little bit and letting my mind wander, and at the end of the recitation the poet alluded to my behaviour.

'I rounded off each section on the triptych with a reflection on romantic love. Although I wasn't in a relationship at the time, I was feeling quite optimistic.'

LAURA ELLIOTT graduated from the UEA Poetry MA in 2012. Her work has been featured in a number of publications including *Tender*, *The White Review*, *3:AM Magazine*, *Berfrois* and *Poetry London*, as well as the Bloodaxe anthology *Dear World and Everyone In It*. She is co-editor of *Lighthouse* literary journal and forthcoming publishing experiment *Paratext*. She lives in South East London and is training to be a librarian.

She writes, '"Skype Blinks" was written in response to the summer edition of the *Postcards* reading series curated last year by Camilla Bostock. This was during a transitional period of my life; I had recently returned from some time in India and moved to London, my sister and her partner started teaching in Vietnam, and other close friends similarly uprooted and left for new cities. In the midst of these separations, presence became an ambiguous and unstable thing, increasingly (necessarily) simulated through mediating systems of digital communication.

'At this particular *Postcards* reading, Camilla projected a poet reading via Skype onto the wall of the studio (a phenomenon that is becoming more and more common but no more technologically fluent) and the contrasts inherent in the layers of framing – the screen, the wall behind it, the windows in the room(s), the act of telling itself, the particularities of light and inevitable disruptions – prompted me to write this poem. At the forefront of the piece is the acknowledgement that these apparent windows can be deceptive: as the polar bear accepts his cell as a tactile compromise, we accept one another in these newly ruptured forms, animated remotely and distracted conceptually. I am led to question how little contact we can take from one another and still derive comfort, how detached are our corporeal narratives, what will we ultimately sacrifice to the allure of proximity.'

MALENE ENGELUND was born in Aalborg, Denmark. Her poems have appeared in a number of magazines and anthologies including *Poetry Wales*, *Magma*, *The Guardian Online*, and she was highly commended in the Faber New Poets scheme 2013-14. She is co-editor of the *Days of Roses* poetry anthologies and lives in London.

She writes, '"The Terns" was written in response to an installation by the German artist Rebecca Horn; here, feathers arranged on mechanised wires take the shape of two wings that continuously fold and unfold over one another. I was drawn to the artwork's strange aesthetics of softness and exactitude and how, in their repetitive movement, these fanned machine-like feathers became a meditation on intimacy and withdrawal.

'"The Terns" is taken from a sequence of poems I am writing from installations and performances by the four artists Ana Mendieta, Rebecca Horn, Louise Bourgeois and Marina Abramovic. While their works differ dramatically in expression and execution, they all share the quality of courage; a fearlessness in engagement and a readiness to expose fallibility at the potential of creating a work of resonance and significance. In writing this sequence, I wanted to avoid any direct descriptive link to the artworks themselves, but instead re-imagine each piece; to carry through the presence it summons and lift the poem to its light.'

RICHARD EVANS grew up in the Staffordshire Moorlands and attended Leicester then Bristol University, where he wrote dissertations on the poetry of Tony Harrison and Simon Armitage. He teaches English and Creative Writing in Kent. He has been selected as a Teacher Trailblazer in Creative Writing by the Poetry Society.

He writes, 'While working with Peter Sansom he introduced me to the "flash fiction" of Dan Rhodes. Rhodes' collection "Anthropology" contains 101 stories about relationships, each of 101 words. *Space Invader* appeared in a subsequent workshop, oddly at almost exactly 101 words. I later saw a student playing "retro" arcade games and the format of *Space Invader* was confirmed. I have always been slightly suspicious of shape poems, but when read aloud I was pleased that the pauses caused by space and lineation added to meaning. My wife, by the way, is fine with the poem: as she rightly observes, I am the one who comes out worse form it! For those of you who know him, it is best read in the voice of Jonny Vegas (try it).'

RUTH FAINLIGHT has published thirteen books of poems, two collections of short stories, and written opera libretti for Covent Garden and Channel 4 TV. Her *New & Collected Poems* appeared at the end of 2010, and her translation of *Sophocles' Theban Plays*, done in collaboration with Robert Littman, came out in 2009. She received the Hawthornden and Cholmondeley Awards in 1994, and her 1997 collection, *Sugar-Paper Blue*, was shortlisted for the 1998 Whitbread Award. Collections of her poems have been published in French, Spanish, Portuguese, Italian and Romanian translation. Ian McMillan, presenter of *The Verb* on Radio 3, chose Ruth Fainlight's *New & Collected Poems* as his "finest poetry offering and his overall best book of the year" in his *Best of 2010* program on the final Radio 2 Book Club of that year.

She writes, 'For months after my husband's death I did not write anything. This began to alarm me: to be deprived of the two most important things in my life at the same time seemed needless cruelty on the part of whatever deity was overseeing my existence. Poems usually announce themselves by an awareness that something I have just written or said belongs to a different category of language than the everyday. If the test of a true poem is the fact that it makes the hair on the back of your neck bristle, the same test applies to the first appearance of a poem to the poet who might be fortunate enough to carry it through to completion. And that is exactly what happened: I was sitting in the passenger seat of a friend's car talking about driving in an area of France we both knew, when I became aware of what I had just said – more or less the first line of my poem – and that numinous feeling came over me. I reached into my bag for a pad and pencil and wrote the words down, and the next weeks were gratefully occupied by what I had feared might never happen again.'

MATTHEW FRANCIS is the author of five poetry collections, of which the latest is *Muscovy* (Faber, 2013). His poetry has twice been shortlisted for the Forward Prize, and in 2004 he was chosen as one of the Next Generation poets. His collection of poems *Micrographia*, inspired by the work of Robert Hooke, is due out from Rufus Books in 2015. He has a particular interest in the early modern period, and his novel *The Book of the Needle* (Cinnamon Press, 2014) is about the seventeenth-century Welsh prophet and tailor Arise Evans. He lives in Wales, and lectures in creative writing at Aberystwyth University.

He writes, 'Robert Hooke's *Micrographia*, an illustrated account of his observations through the microscope, was perhaps the first popular science book. Samuel Pepys rushed out to get an advance copy from his bookseller and stayed up till two o'clock in the morning reading it; it was, he wrote, "the most ingenious book I ever read in my life". Hooke describes insects and plants, feathers and fish scales – even the edge of a razor or the point of a needle were excitingly different from this new perspective. His illustrations, including fold-out depictions of a fearsome-looking flea and louse, are fascinating, as is the quirky and charming prose of his descriptions. I have long been fascinated by visionaries, and Hooke, the friend and collaborator of Wren and Boyle, rival and enemy of Newton, is as much a visionary as a scientist in the modern sense. Part of the charm of reading him is the process of thinking oneself into his historical world with its still slightly blurred categories, where a silverfish can be both bookworm and moth, while a moth, covered in "feathers" becomes a kind of miniature bird. My poem like many of those in the sequence, adapts and condenses two of Hooke's observations.'

CLAUDIA FRIEDRICH was born in 1989 in Germany. She studied Creative Writing and graduated in 2012 from Liverpool's John Moores University. She translates German poets and writes about her family's history and political issues in her country. She also published *In the Red 10*, Liverpool's Literature Magazine. She now lives in Rostock, Germany.

She writes, 'In 2011, the dissertation of Karl Theodor Maria Nikolaus Johann Jakob Philipp Franz Joseph Sylvester Freiherr von und zu Guttenberg, Minister of Defence in Germany, was exposed as plagiarism. On average, every third word was taken from newspaper articles or scientific papers. Using his rejection speech from February 2011, I copied every third word and translated it into English. Within two weeks, the incident lead to his resignation and the loss of his PhD. The original German text is taken from www.sueddeutsche.de, 18.02.2011.'

MATTHEW GREGORY was born in Suffolk, 1984, and studied at the Norwich School of Art & Design and Goldsmiths College, where he is researching a PhD. He has lived in Prague, New York, St Petersburg and Naples. His poems have appeared in national publications and anthologies since 2005, including the *London Review of Books*, *The White Review*, *Poetry London*, *Poetry Review* and Salt's *The Best British Poetry 2011* and *2013* and Bloodaxe's *Dear World & Everyone In It*. His work has been aired on BBC radio. In 2010, he received an Eric Gregory award.

He writes, 'The note accompanying this poem at the foot of my sequence, Rooms, states "The Grand Hotel des Roches Noires, in Trouville-sur-Mer, Normandy, was a glamorous hub for the sporting and gambling sets of the early 20th century, falling into decline years later." There's little I'd add to that with regards to the subject matter. More interesting to me was how, in writing it, I became aware of some general notions on the genesis and composition of my poems. How it was necessary to let a sort of revolving table of images, sensory "apparitions" and soluble concepts cycle through me for a period, until the most visible of them began to suggest a palette and the "secondary" or "tertiary" elements a texture in which to foreground the dominant shades. From this alloy, insubstantial, unstable, the poem began to distil. I realised that my method was coming quite close to a visual art – not exactly painterly or cinematic but with something of both in tendency. What emerged in writing was something that wasn't exactly a visual filter or admixture, but a particular unrendered quality, unique to its medium – a type of light gradient that would also have to be sonic, the quiet press of interior spaces on the line, and an elegiac lustre to everything else. These airs or atmospheres began to take precedence as aesthetic "constraints", above any formal ones, and it was in translating them into lyrics that the *Rooms* sequence began to define itself. I recently read some interviews with the film editor Walter Murch, who talked about the organic palette of a movie – for instance, the continuation of a "green" note through a film or how the slightest bell tolling in the third scene could alter the complexion of a girl sunbathing in the fifth. These balancing acts seem very close to my preoccupation in a single poem, in a series.'

DAVID HARSENT's *Legion* won the Forward Prize for best collection 2005; *Night* (2011) won the Griffin International Poetry Prize and was triple short-listed in the UK. *In Secret*, his English versions of poems by Yannis Ritsos, was a PBS Translation Choice. A new collection – *Fire Songs* – appeared from Faber in August 2014. Harsent has collaborated with composers – most often with Harrison Birtwistle – on commissions that have been performed at venues world-wide, including the Royal Opera House, the Proms, the Concertgebouw, the South Bank Centre, the Aldeburgh Festival, The Salzburg Festival, the Bregenz Festival, and Carnegie Hall. He is Professor of Creative Writing at the University of Roehampton.

He writes, '"Fire: *end-scenes and outtakes*" is one of the four "Fire Songs" that form the superstructure of my most recent collection. I went on retreat to work on what I thought was a long poem in progress: working title, "Fire". When I returned, I had four somewhat shorter poems, two finished, two in progress. The other poems in the collection in some way refer to these four poems, or borrow from them, or reflect them, or expand on some aspect of them (and that didn't happen by design). Throughout, the narrative substance of the book is fictional.

'Back-story: a man goes into his garden and builds a bonfire on which he plans to burn everything – letters, diaries, notebooks, photos, mementos . . . I might have been thinking of Larkin's death-bed instruction: "Burn everything." (Did he really say that, or do I want him to have said it?) The fire reminds the man of other fires – "heretics" burned, cities sacked, war-zones ablaze, hints of the heat-death of the planet; or he sees shapes in the fire that remind him of his past: of what's being sent to the fire.

'The events noted in this poem are either versions of the actual or are illustrative. The occasional sections given in italics under the heading "Notebook" are simply that: notes made on certain subjects and now called into use. It might be, I suppose, that those notebooks are among the items to be burned.'

LEE HARWOOD, born 1939, has spent much of his life by the sea in Brighton, Sussex. His most recent books were *Collected Poems* (2004), *Selected Poems* (2008) – both published by Shearsman Books – and *The Orchid Boat* (2014, Enitharmon Press).

He writes, 'Beside other concerns the poem is essentially about respect for the "little people" – people you pass in the street, people who serve you in shops or a Post Office – to remember and think of their stories and trials. It's about the stoicism and decency of a generation that's now disappearing, but who taught us so much. It's about getting through.'

OLI HAZZARD, first book, *Between Two Windows*, published by Carcanet in 2012, won the Michael Murphy Prize for a first collection of poems and an Eric Gregory Award from the Society of Authors. A pamphlet of prose poems, *Within Habit*, was published by Test Centre earlier this year. He is currently a DPhil student at Wolfson College, Oxford.

He writes, 'The sequence this poem is taken from was originally called *Eclogues*, and though the title later changed to *Within Habit*, some ecloguey properties remain. Meliboeus, who is addressed at the end of this poem, is the name of a character in Virgil's *Eclogues*. And the word "eclogue" derives from the Greek ἐκλέγειν, "to select", which more or less describes the compositional processes I used: the vast majority of the text was found on the internet, copied into a word document, cut up, then inserted into the poems, where further selections and alterations would occur. Each of the 20 poems in the sequence uses the same form as the one included here: two banks of prose – broken and mended internally by vertical lines – connected by a single word or phrase. This approach developed accidentally and I liked it for a couple of reasons. It asked some questions about the relationship between poems and prose poems I didn't and still don't know the answers to. It also seemed to generate a kind of tension between two perspectives: one from which the poems are considered as images –

that is, as though they were somehow not constituted of language, as you can look down upon a landscape from a plane or a computer screen and view it not as fields or streets, but as an abstract pattern – and another, "street-view" experience of them, moving linearly through the text, over and through the words and dividing lines. I sometimes think of these lines as marking the point where enjambment has occurred in another poem, like a piece of paper that has been folded then unfolded back into its original state, leaving only a remnant of the gesture. Sometimes they function like parentheses; sometimes they abruptly curtail speech; sometimes they allow for random phrases to be placed in sequence, like the peculiar fruits of the fruit machine: *pineapple, 7, bar.*'

SARAH HOWE was born in Hong Kong in 1983. Her Tall-lighthouse pamphlet, *A Certain Chinese Encyclopedia*, won an Eric Gregory Award in 2010. Her work appears in *The Salt Book of Younger Poets* (Salt, 2011), *Dear World & Everyone In It* (Bloodaxe, 2013) and *Ten: The New Wave* (Bloodaxe, 2014). She is a Research Fellow at Gonville and Caius College, Cambridge. Her first collection is forthcoming from Chatto & Windus in 2015.

She writes, 'I wrote "A loop of jade" during a month's residency at Hawthornden Castle, which turned out to be the most focused and prolific period of writing I've ever experienced. About a third of what will become my first book emerged that crisp January in 2012. This poem felt like it arose out of a series of intuitive formal decisions. I'd been thinking about hybrid prose-verse forms such as the *haibun* – the different voices offered by the shift in and out of lineation. I had also been reading Edmund de Waal's *The Hare with Amber Eyes*. I was impressed by the way it wove its many histories around his inherited *netsuke*: how those carved wooden figures felt rolled around the palm, the way their tactile reality provided – or seemed to – an emotional connection to the past. I wanted to think about lines of inheritance, searched-for roots, but also things one might not want to pass on. The jade bracelet my grandmother gave me as a baby seemed as apt an emblem as I'd find. I have no memory of her. The important things in the poem are left unsaid: the fact, for example, that she wasn't actually my grandmother by blood, but the woman who rather tenuously took in my mother as an abandoned baby in Guangdong. The bracelet has always felt to me like something out of a fairy tale – the sort of token that instigates the creakily plotted recognition scene, when the foundling heir is finally reunited with his or her true family. I wear it to readings sometimes, on its watch chain.'

CAOILINN HUGHES' first collection of poetry, *Gathering Evidence*, was published by Carcanet Press in 2014. A group of twenty poems from the collection won the 2012 Patrick Kavanagh Award, among several other prizes. She recently moved from New Zealand to The Netherlands, where she is an Assistant Professor at Maastricht University. She also writes fiction.

She writes, 'Boys are meant to deconstruct radios and to put them back together, to make something that functions. Girls are meant to slit open daisy stems and connect the flowers, to make something that charms, or adorns. Perhaps this poem takes apart a daisy chain and reassembles it as a radio.

'If not, perhaps it goes some way to breaking down how we perceive an entity like a daisy chain, trying to understand its nature, once aesthetic ideals, social contexts, spiritual ramifications and other ascribed meanings are peeled away. In some senses, it's a coming to terms with the daisy chain.

'If not, perhaps it merely mirrors a pretty, if unfathomable, pattern. It borrows the end-rhymes and the quatrain structure of a pantoum, without repeating whole phrases. The rhyme scheme is something like the below. Genomic!'

> Stanza 1: A B C D
> Stanza 2: B E D F
> Stanza 3: E G F H
> Stanza 4: G I H J
> Stanza 5: I I

KIRSTEN IRVING is one of the two editors behind collaborative poetry press Sidekick Books. Her publications include *What To Do* (Happenstance, 2011) and *Never Never Never Come Back* (Salt Publishing, 2012). Her work has featured in anthologies on science fiction, poetic form, the Simpsons and David Lynch's *Blue Velvet*, and she is currently working on her first show and a steampunk novel. Kirsten lives in London, where she works as a freelance copywriter and proofreader.

She writes, 'The title of "No fish are we now" came from a misheard Al Stewart lyric, and from that false foundation I wanted to write a piece that gradually, evenly fell apart. There was an element of gameplay in the ever-depleting inventory. Influenced by such adventure narratives as *Moby-Dick* and *Aguirre*, in which monomaniacal quests completely go to pieces in hostile terrain, I chose to set it in the ocean. Isolation, a blurring of myth and reality (especially under the influence of sickness, stress or thirst) and countless ways to die made it the perfect frame. Using short, calm stanzas I wanted to mimic the waves and the relentless drift towards disaster.'

ALAN JENKINS was born in 1955 and has lived for most of his life in London. He is Deputy Editor and Poetry Editor at the *TLS*, and has taught creative writing in the USA, London and Paris. His collections of poetry include, most recently, *A Shorter Life* (2005) and *Revenants* (2013); *Drunken Boats*, containing his acclaimed translation of Rimbaud's "Le Bateau ivre", was published in 2007, and *Blue Days* (The Sailor's Return) in 2010. *A Short History of Snakes*, selected poems, was published in 2001 by Grove Press, New York. He is a Fellow of the Royal Society of Literature.

He writes, 'My mother's father died when I was two, but his presence or absence cast a long shadow over our household. He plays an unresolved part in my family romance: a certain kind of pre-war Englishman, resourceful, authoritarian, nautically inclined, perhaps a bit of a chancer, the sort who, though they didn't exactly build or serve the Empire, hoped to make their fortunes from it. At my school, which was founded after the First World War to educate the fatherless sons of drowned merchant seamen, I encountered a very different kind of sea-dog, crackling with anger and bitterness beneath the naval discipline. Deptford was once synonymous with the English seafaring spirit, and the shore-life of sailors that went with it. Christopher Marlowe was killed there, and Conrad's Marlow has passed it countless times on his way up or downriver. "Hunters for gold or pursuers of fame, they all had gone out on that stream. . . ." I lived there, on the border with its smarter neighbour Royal Greenwich, for a while in the 1970s and 80s, and the poem started with a night two years ago when I found myself revisiting old haunts around the time of the Queen's Diamond Jubilee – she had just officially launched the royal barge *Gloriana*.'

MIMI KHALVATI has published eight collections with Carcanet Press, including *Child: New & Selected Poems*, a Poetry Book Society Special Commendation, and *The Meanest Flower*, shortlisted for the T.S. Eliot Prize. She is the founder of The Poetry School where she teaches. She has received a Cholmondeley Award, a major Arts Council Writer's Award and is a Fellow of the Royal Society of Literature. Her new collection, *The Weather Wheel*, is a Poetry Book Society Recommendation.

She writes, 'This poem appears in my book *The Weather Wheel*, in which all the poems, often taking weather as the starting point, are in eight free verse couplets, with something reminiscent of the sonnet, something of the ghazal. Reading the last of Nabokov's early Russian novels in English, *Glory* (from which I quote), started me thinking about what it is that I read novels for – not for plot or story but for those moments of illumination that diffuse a kind of starlight around you wherever you go – to a café in Covent Garden, a poetry reading on Upper Street where, escaping for a smoke, you stare up into the Christmas lights. My favourite authors – Virginia Woolf, Proust – seem to litter every page with these sparks, scintillas, where I would count myself lucky to have even one on one.

'Reflecting the sonnet's turn, "Bringing Down the Stars" was written in two parts, at different times. The "sestet" gave me particular trouble, trying to find the right connecting thought in a changed syntax, and has ended up as a long breathless exclamatory rush. I dithered endlessly over the punctuation and in the end kept it to a minimum. The mouse appears since there are other mice, rats, small creatures in my collection, that pop up when they feel like it – on this occasion, rather to my surprise, in my person. Incidentally, the poem was written long before Yalta was in the news which of course has cast a grimmer, sadder light on it and pushed its own diamond lights further back into the past.'

HANNAH LOWE's first collection *Chick* (Bloodaxe, 2013) was shortlisted for the Forward Best First Collection Prize and the Aldeburgh Fenton Best First Collection Prize. Her pamphlet, *Ormonde* (Hercules Editions) is forthcoming in November. Her memoir *Long Time, No See* (Periscope) is due in Spring 2015.

She writes, '"The Other Family" has its genesis in a Super 8 film my half-brother showed me of him and my father play-boxing in the garden of his childhood home, in the early 1960s. It shows my father as a relatively young man – younger than I'd even seen him in photographs – although in fact it wasn't his first marriage. There was another other family before the one in the film.

'I'd only known my father as an old man, so the film's images really struck me – my father's physical agility and my half-brother's eagerness, the shy smile – he looks so keen to please. The film pulled me back into time, and so the poem plays with the idea of filmic time – the sense of rewinding, frame by frame, and its structure – the short, enjambed lines – is meant to reflect this. Time was always a strange commodity for my father, since he played cards all night. It's entirely possible that he'd been up all night, and is play-boxing with his son in the early morning sunshine, before going up to bed.

'There's an edginess to that film I hope I've captured in the poem. I explore the relationships of men, whether familial or friendships, through-out the collection this poem comes from. My father's own upbringing was violent and neglectful, and I wanted the poem to explore how he related to his own son. There's love and attention, but the boxing is tinged with the threat of real violence – the punches don't connect, but they could.

'Through the context of the collection you know my father is a gambler and an immigrant. I hope the poem's last line "coming home with what you know" makes the reader think about what a man like this might know – how to earn money is one thing; how to live and survive in a hostile country might be another; and how to be a certain type of husband and father, a certain type of man.'

LYDIA MACPHERSON was born in 1961 in Yorkshire and lives near Cambridge and in Winchester. Her first collection, *Love Me Do* (Salt, 2014), won the Crashaw Prize in 2013.

She writes, 'I started writing poetry in 2005 and had a period of intense creativity for about five years. I was diagnosed with bipolar disorder in 2009 and almost as soon as I started the medication for this, the poetry stopped. Instead of the highs and lows, which were hard but fruitful, life was flat. Safer, but chemically coshed. A friend suggested I write about how that felt and *Lithium Lovesong* is the result.

'The poem started with the periodic table and went from there. I wanted to get a tone of both ownership of the situation ('my element') and submission to it. I was intrigued by the properties of lithium: despite its stony name it is the least dense metal and is found in sea water. The sea images came easily as so much of life with lithium does feel like moving through an unfamiliar element which cuts me off from the world. Lowell's "a little salt in my brain" was in my brain too and Prufrock's pair of ragged claws were waving at me from the sea bed.

'I've lived the flattened life for five years now and have recently decided to say goodbye to lithium and take my chances with highs, lows and hopefully more poetry.

'*Lithium Lovesong* was commended in the Poetry on the Lake Prize 2011 and in the Forward Prize 2014.'

GLYN MAXWELL's last book of poems was *Pluto*, which was shortlisted for the Forward Prize. In 2012 he published his best-selling guidebook *On Poetry*. He is currently at work on *Nothing*, a libretto for the Royal Opera House and Glyndebourne; on *The City of Tomorrow* for Radio 4, a play about his home-town, the idealistic "garden city" Welwyn, which forms part of the centenary homage to Dylan Thomas; and on a production draft of *The Beast in the Jungle*, a screenplay based on the Henry James novella. He recently quit working at the University of Essex, and now teaches at the new Live Canon Academy.

He writes, 'This poem is one of a recent group that draw their titles from the words of Poor Tom in *King Lear*. Others include "Warm Thee" (about benefit cuts) "Ratsbane" (about a drug deal) and "Pillycock" (about the general bullshit). The poems – in contrast to those in *Pluto* – are intended to be outward-looking, songlike, concerned with England. Modu and Mahu, shadowy looming powers in the mind of Poor Tom (or Edgar as he plays Poor Tom) are here reimagined as superstar comedians, whose unions and dissolutions make the evening news. I don't quite understand how our culture reached the point where the thoughts and feelings of stand-up comics – male ones, mostly – loom this large, but the poem is not exaggerating. Perhaps the unsaid plangent thing is that poets might be worth a hearing, but never mind . . . My theory is that the currency of stand-up is *digital* – if we laugh it's a 1, if we don't it's a 0 – which fits very well into the streamlined simple-minded body politic, in a way that poets, with our perplexing *analogue*, our unquantifiable fractions and cosines, never could. So it's okay to laugh at the disabled, or poke fun at the unusual, or abuse womanhood, as long as someone's laughing. What a filthy cargo's come in on the good ship *Banter*. What the fuck is going on with *men?*'

CHRIS MCCABE's collections are *The Hutton Inquiry*, *Zeppelins*, *THE RESTRUCTURE* and *Speculatrix*, published in December 2014 by Penned in the Margins. He has recorded a CD with the Poetry Archive and was shortlisted for The Ted Hughes Award in 2014. His plays *Shad Thames*, *Broken Wharf* and *Mudflats* have been performed in London and Liverpool and he has written a book of prose, *In the Catacombs: a summer among the dead poets of West Norwood Cemetery*. He works as the Poetry Librarian at The Saison Poetry Library and teaches for The Poetry School.

He writes, '"The Duchess of Malfi" is one of a sequence of nine poems inspired by Jacobean drama, each of which has the title of a specific play. Each poem is spoken through the voice of a spurned or aspiring lover and is set at the point of the play's first London performance, at the location of that playhouse. I took the notion of imagining the original players dragging their character roles onto the streets and playing out the emotions for real, for themselves, forgetting that their words are supposed to be a theatrical conceit. I also experimented with anachronistic language, that is: I gave the characters free-reign to plunder the current vernacular of late capitalism and to use that language as a way to illustrate their various disillusionments and anger. This anachronism works in reverse too, allowing me to mine the often cryptic and compressed pre-dictionary language of the poet-playwrights to explore the political backdrop of contemporary London. These prose sonnets in sprung rhythm are published as a whole in my collection *Speculatrix* (Penned in the Margins, 2014).'

CHRISTOPHER MIDDLETON was born in Cornwall in 1926. After studying at Merton College, Oxford, he held academic positions at the University of Zurich and King's College London. In 1966 he took up a position as Professor of Germanic Languages & Literature at the University of Texas, Austin, from which he retired in 1998.

He has published translations of Robert Walser, Nietzsche, Holder-lïn, Goethe, Gert Hofmann and many others, as well as 30 books of poetry, the most recent of which is *Collected Later Poems* (Carcanet, 2014).

ANDREW MOTION was Poet Laureate from 1999 to 2009 and is co-founder and co-director of the Poetry Archive. He is Professor of Creative Writing at Royal Holloway College, University of London.

He writes, 'When I was born my parents were living in a converted mill in Hertfordshire, but as soon as my brother and I were old enough to fall into the mill-stream they moved north into Essex – into a house opposite a mill. This mill, still working, with an enormous miller who occasionally appeared in the front door of his building like a ghost, was off limits to us. My mother thought we might get squashed crossing the lane to go there, and maybe also thought we'd get turned into bread (fe, fi, fo, fum) if we made it. This of course made the place very alarming to us but very appealing as well. My poem is about the mill, and about how when I look back to it now I can hardly believe that my childhood was indeed mine.'

ANDRÉ NAFFIS-SAHELY's poetry was most recently featured in the *Oxford Poets Anthology 2013* (Carcanet Press). His translations include *The Physiology of the Employee* by Honoré de Balzac (Wakefield Press, 2014), *Money* by Émile Zola (Penguin Classics, 2015) and *The Selected Poems* of Abdellatif Laâbi (Carcanet Press, 2015).

He writes, 'This poem was penned in March 2014 while I was travel-ling across the United States on Amtrak, the first leg of which included taking the California Zephyr from Sacramento to Chicago. Alongside this poem, I also produced a travelogue where I wrote: "Trains have the unique ability to pick up passengers according to roughly regular sched-ules and then take them slightly outside of time. Thus, the inner self is uncorked: you find yourself telling strangers about that girl you lost your mind over, that second husband you should never have married, that wild night you had with your best friend. Trains become stranger-free zones."'

JOHN NORTH. Poet. Writer. Born in the north of England in 1990. Awarded the degree of Master of Arts with Distinction at the University of Manchester in 2012, after graduating with a BA (Hons) in 2011. Poems can be found in *The Fire Crane*, *The North*, *Kaffeeklatsch*, *The Interpreter's House*, *CAST: The Poetry Business Book of New Contemporary Poets*, *The Manchester Review* and *Boston Poetry Magazine*.

He writes, 'I was in the garden I began writing the poem in, again, just the other day. It is the kind of garden that catches colour, like a stained glass window, in leaves, plants, flowers, cupped by a hedge on top of a low, knee-height dry stone wall. I spent a lot of time in that garden as a child. I have spent a lot of time in that garden as a young man. Through good times and bad. Time passes. A garden changes. But it is still the same garden I was in as a child, even if I now see it from a greater height, with a changed mind.

'What is the poem about? Maybe hope and hopelessness. A not-certain point in life. Seeing the world. Trying to hold it.

'I needed to write it down. Maybe the poem is about needing to write it down, me personally needing to write it down. Maybe it is about humans needing to write it down, from things on cave walls onwards.

'The world outside the body. The body. The world with the body. A moment.

'I will write more poems about that garden.'

RUTH PADEL's most recent collection, *Learning to Make an Oud in Nazareth*, is a meditation on conflict, creativity and the Middle East. She has published ten collections, a novel, and a range of non-fiction including books on reading contemporary poetry and studies of ancient Greek poetry and tragedy. Awards include First Prize in the National Poetry Competition, Cholmondeley Award for poetry and a British Council Darwin Now research award. She is Fellow of the Royal Society of Literature and Poetry Fellow at King's College London. www.ruthpadel.com

She writes, 'Twenty years ago on a reading tour in Palestine and Israel I visited the Art section of Yad Vashem's Holocaust History Museum. I spent a long time with a chain carved out of wooden broom-handle, which had scenes of life in a detention camp incised on the links. It was made in a French-run Nazi camp by Moshe ("Max") Scheiner, a Polish Jew living in France and arrested in 1941. He made it there and gave the chain to his wife. In 1942 he was deported to Auschwitz-Birkenau where he died. Years later, I realized I had to write about this. The poem became a kind of companion piece to the title poem about making an oud, the iconic Arabic musical instrument, which quotes from The Song of Solomon. Quotes in "The Chain" are from the Psalms. The Museum kindly sent me a photograph to refresh my memory of the chain and allowed me to reproduce this in my collection *Learning to Make an Oud in Nazareth* whose theme is craftsmanship, creativity and conflict and whose last line is "making is our defence against the dark".'

ABIGAIL PARRY lives and works in London, and has recently completed a PhD on wordplay in contemporary poetry. She received an Eric Gregory Award in 2010.

She writes, 'I don't really have very much to say about this. I'm attracted to poems about transgression, particularly when they feature smooth-talking animals, and particularly when the poem's on the side of the transgression. I suppose the vocabulary and imagery are fairly phallic, but this was never intended to be an overtly sexual poem – it's about curiosity. When I was younger, the adult world seemed simultaneously very exciting, and very full of ominous silences. The poem deals in both these things.'

CHRISTOPHER RIESCO lives in Manchester and works in Salford. Through good fortune and the patience of others he was able to attend the Writing School at Manchester Metropolitan University. He hopes no-one builds anything on the empty ground at Pomona.

He writes, 'The title for this poem came to me when I was walking along next to a grey wall, and I worked from the title outward. It was not so much that I wanted to give Caliban's version, but that the island does look different from different angles. This angle is not pleasant, but we cannot be too pleasant about the island seeing as we cannot leave.

'I do not know if it is a true dramatic monologue. Anyway, haven't Caliban's already been written? I do hope, however, that anyone who likes the poem might then see about writing a poem which is not "what I say" but "what someone would say". I find that most good poems, anyway, whether or not they express, create, and that whether or not they say something, they do something.'

CAROL RUMENS' most recent collection of poems is *De Chirico's Threads* (Seren, 2010). She teaches Creative Writing at the University of Bangor. She also writes fiction, plays and literary journalism. She was born in Forest Hill, South London, in December 1944.

She writes, 'Attila József (1905-1937) was born in a run-down district of Budapest, the son of a washer-woman and a soap-factory-worker. The father abandoned his wife and children when Attila was three. The boy experienced much trauma and deprivation, but a wealthy brother-in-law helped him later to establish a career. Attila published his first collection at 17, and is regarded as Hungary's foremost poet. His death under a train in a tunnel near Lake Balaton was probably suicide.

'In 2013, the Hungarian Cultural Institute, London, asked some British poets to respond to poems by Attila József for an anthology to be launched on the poet's birthday, April 11th. "Easter Snow" isn't the poem published in the anthology: it's a spin-off. I was going to add "from the research" but that's too pretentious a description of my random reading. I borrowed a passport (surrealism) and went wandering through the poet's life and locations – including an online astrological chart I found for his birthdate! I don't have any Hungarian, but I read a lot of Attila's translated poems. Even in sometimes quite awkward-sounding English versions, they shine fresh as wet ink. They are political, visionary, rich in ideas and feeling – vibrantly the work of the whole man.

'I mixed these glimpses into the metre of my favourite English nursery-rhyme, "There was a man of double deed", adding a quote or a direct allusion here and there, and imagery of my own. It's a kind of lullaby to the fatherless child-poet. I see its shape as a tall apartment block, with a small courtyard, and a window where the child peers out, plotting his flight. In the poem quoted in the second epigraph, death is Attila's "native country". In "Easter Snow", it is and it isn't.'

DECLAN RYAN was born in Co. Mayo, Ireland and lives in north London. He co-edits the *Days of Roses* anthology series and is poetry editor at *Ambit*. He is working on a PhD on "perfect speech" in Ian Hamilton's poems at Royal Holloway, and teaches poetry at King's College London. His debut pamphlet was recently published in the Faber New Poets series.

He writes, 'This comes from the early part of a series to do with boxing I've been writing for a while, with a working title "Slow guitar, soft trumpet and a bell": a quote by Sonny Liston about what a "blues song for fighters" would be called. The sequence tracks a number of these men from their unbeatable, godlike state through first losses, degenerations and – in some cases – resurrection stories. There are few exceptions to the trajectory from prospect to opponent for the following generation of prospects. I'm a fan of the sport for its own merits, but I also like that one of the key enemies of a fighter is self-awareness. Also that one can't train for six months, cut away every ounce of extraneous flesh and stand in a ring for twelve rounds as blows are aimed at your head only to say afterwards "I didn't mean it." It seems to me a noble thing to put oneself in a position where if you fail you can't pretend you set out to do so, or that failure isn't possible. Linked to all this is a quote Ian Hamilton prefaced his biography of Matthew Arnold with, from Arnold's notebooks, "It is a sad thing to see a man who has been frittered away piecemeal by petty distractions, and who has never done his best. But it is still sadder to see a man who has done his best, who has reached his utmost limits – and finds his work a failure, and himself far less than he had imagined himself." I think something in that quote helps to explain why fighters embrace after the bell, and tend to pay for each other's funerals.'

RICHARD SCOTT was born in London in 1981 and was educated at The Royal College of Music, The Faber Academy and Goldsmiths College, London. His poetry has been published in *Poetry Review*, *Poetry London*,

Magma, Rialto and *Wasafiri* magazines. Richard's work has also been included in *The Poetry of Sex*, a Penguin Anthology and *In Protest: 150 Poems for Human Rights*. Richard also writes and presents a weekly radio show about opera and libretti, entitled *The Opera Hour*, on Resonance 104.4FM. Richard has written on poetry, opera and libretti for *The Guardian*, *The Arts Desk*, *The Quietus* and *Poetry News*.

He writes, '"Pilgrimage" is really about my good friend Sam who is attracted to men that look like Jesus – tanned men with beards and flowing locks, usually sporting a six-pack. This was something I could never understand exactly until he took me to see at exhibition of altar pieces and devotional items from The Spanish Golden Age.

'These meticulously carved life-sized figures, often incorporating ivory teeth, real eye lashes and hair, eyes varnished with egg whites to look wet and alive, made a real impression on me. Especially as they were often made for private devotion – nuns and kings alike would pray for hours in front of these sensual, near-naked, bruised and bloodied statues of Jesus within the intimacy of their private chapels.

'"Pilgrimage" originally tried to capture Sam's feelings in the gallery, observing these devout yet intensely sexual objects but I could never quite make it work until I re-situated the poem into a gay bar and included all the intensity and spontaneity of a sexual encounter that might take place there.

'"Pilgrimage" is a short poem because in spite of all the desire and devotion behind it, the sexual encounter is by necessity, short lived and breathless. It also blends religious iconography – after Sam's initial obsession with Jesus, which takes him into the cubicle, he becomes fascinated with his lover's tattoo which is more about The Old Testament narrative of Noah.

'I wanted the reader to really see the tattoo and feel the heady drunken confusion of kissing a Jesus look-a-like whilst finding Noah's dove inked on his stomach. I wanted the reader to look again at the figure and body of Jesus. I wanted sexuality and the male physique to permeate the sacred and the poetic. I wanted the reader to place themselves into Sam's shoes – indeed the second stanza is almost a list of instructions should the reader ever find themselves in a similar situation . . .'

IAN SEED is editor of www.shadowtrain.com. His publications include *Makers of Empty Dreams* (Shearsman, 2014), *Sleeping with the Ice Cream Vendor* (KF&S, 2012), *Threadbare Fables* (LikeThisPress, 2012), *Amore Mio* (Flax, 2011), *Shifting Registers* (Shearsman, 2011), *the straw which comes apart* (translations from the Italian of Ivano Fermini) (Oystercatcher Press, 2010), and *Anonymous Intruder* (Shearsman, 2009). He teaches at the University of Chester.

He writes, '"Prize-Giving" comes from a book-length series of prose poems (*Makers of Empty Dreams*), many of them with a relationship to Italy, a country where I lived for ten years. My prose poems seek to disturb, enchant and amuse, though I as the author do not have this in mind when I start to write. I work a lot from dreams and very early morning writing, when I am still open to a different kind of reality. Key influences are Kafka (of course), Max Jacob, Pierre Reverdy, and the little-known British poet Cory Harding.

'In 2011/12, I was writing up my PhD thesis on the Italian author Beppe Fenoglio. The backlash – perhaps as a kind of reaction to the way I had to marshal my ideas into a coherent whole for my thesis – was that I would wake up in the night with all kinds of odd fragments of images and narratives floating around in my head. Five or ten minutes was all it took to write these down. Once or twice a week I would re-visit them and see if I could find something which, with some tinkering, splicing and building, might be of interest to a reader. I think the fact that I had very little time pushed the writing into a kind of brevity, vividness and immediacy which I had always striven for, but previously found difficult to achieve. For the rest, I believe that "Prize-Giving" speaks for itself.'

MARTHA SPRACKLAND grew up on Merseyside and lived in Madrid before taking an MA at Lancaster University. Twice a Foyle Young Poet of the Year, her work has appeared in various places, including *Poetry Review*, *London Review of Books*, *Poetry London*, and the *Salt Book of Younger Poets*. She was co-founder and Poetry Editor of *Cake* magazine, and is now Assistant Poetry Editor for Faber & Faber.

She writes, 'This poem is one of a handful of poems I wrote very close together, about extraordinary scientific accidents, freak weather events, and the people who survive them (my mum once referred to this sequence as "your unfortunate men", which I think is entirely a good thing). This was the first, and in many ways the manifesto for the whole project.

'When my brother and I were young we were obsessed with the Guinness Book of Records, and this is the story that stuck with me most. Roy "Dooms" Sullivan was, over the space of about forty years, struck by lightning seven times, surviving each and eventually dying by his own hand. His story is pretty well-known, but what interested me was that first childhood incident, which seems to me the most important, but which was excluded from the records. I feel like that last stanza is a little glimpse of what it's all about – the accepted explanation for Sullivan's life was that he was a ranger in the National Park, and thereby simply exposed to lightning more than your average person. And that must be true, of course, to some extent. But that first strike, in field, as a child, falls outside everything, was the beginning of this extraordinary story, yet is cut.

'His obituary contained my favourite line – too good to put in the poem, really – that Sullivan had taken his own life as the result of "troubles unrelated to lightning". As if everything else is, somehow, about lightning.'

JULIAN STANNARD is a Reader in Creative Writing at the University of Winchester. He is the author of *Rina's War* (Peterloo 2001), *The Red Zone* (Peterloo, 2007), *The Parrots of Villa Gruber Discover Lapis Lazuli* (Salmon, 2011) and *The Street of Perfect Love* (Worple Press, 2014). He co-edited *The Palm Beach Effect: Reflections on Michael Hofmann* (CB Editions, 2013). He reviews for the *TLS*.

He writes, 'The poem came after reading a newspaper article about the outbreak of war – no precise recollections apart from a strange and rather alluring sense of quiet – the lull before the storm. The poem came quickly without a great deal of revision. Only after I'd written it did I think of Auden's "September 1 1939" – "We must love one another or die" – but perhaps at some level I'd been thinking of it all along.'

JON STONE was born in Derby and lives in London. His poems have appeared in anthologies of imitation, formal innovation, science fiction, erotic and comic book poetry. *School of Forgery* (Salt, 2012) brings all these elements together, while he also collates, collaborates and anthologises through Sidekick Books, the small press he runs with Kirsten Irving. He won a Society of Authors Eric Gregory Award in 2012 and the *Poetry London* competition in 2014.

He writes, '*Endings* . . . is a computer game poem that didn't make it into (and wasn't intended for) *Coin Opera 2: Fulminare's Revenge*, the treasury of computer game poems I edited with Kirsty last year. It tracks an infamous cut-scene from *Final Fantasy VII*. But it was actually written as part of a whole sequence called "Endings to Adventure Gamebooks" – about twelve poems long and counting – which describe the deaths of various real and fictional characters as if they were one of the "bad" endings to a Choose Your Own Adventure novel. The rhyme-scheme is something I call "creeping rhyme" – it shifts slowly, via vowel, consonant, hard, soft and fuzzy rhymes, over the course of the poem. In every poem in this sequence, the rhyme moves inexorably toward the word "over", as we all move by increments towards our ultimate end.'

TODD SWIFT was born in Montreal, Canada in 1966 and has lived in England since 2003. He now holds dual Canadian-British citizenship. His *Selected Poems* is from Marick Press, USA, 2014. He is the author of eight previous poetry collections. He has edited and co-edited many anthologies. He holds a PhD from UEA, and is Senior Lecturer in Creative

Writing at The University of Worcester. His poems and reviews have appeared widely in places such as *Poetry London* and *Poetry* (Chicago). In 2004 he was Oxfam GB's Poet-in-residence. He is Director of Eyewear Publishing Ltd.

He writes, 'This poem was originally written after a call for poems on the theme or subject of "Red Shoes" – which for me (as I imagine for most) conjures up images of that great, lurid and melodramatic British film from the late 1940s, based on a Hans Christian Andersen fairy tale. The film's story involves a young female ballet dancer who is ambitious, and her Svengali-like mentor, the impresario Lermontov. Love and artistic tensions ensue, and, tragically, in the end, the dancer kills herself, leaving the stage bereft. Victoria's adept body and creative prowess enthrall and intrigue various men who seek to master her, usually through some form of aesthetic domination, to which, until the triumphant/ doomed end, she more or less submits. Needless to say, then, images and ideas relating to submission, the erotic nature of teaching, the trying nature of art, dance, desire, and deviancy, are all gestured at in the film, which is also an example of the "Forties Style" of quasi-camp flamboyance I enjoy in poetry of the period. For numerous reasons relating to temperament, and personality, I sometimes write poems inspired by the movies; and find myself drawn to themes that explore "queerness', however subtly – like Larkin before me I am a "lesbian" manqué (that is, in my fantasy world I am sometimes a stylish woman in love with stylish women).

'As a married Catholic man, I am following in the footsteps of the married Catholic poet F.T. Prince, who explored aspects of queer desire in his poetry of the 1940s, often flamboyant rhetorically. I am, in this poem, figured as the master and the slave, the teacher and the student, the mentor and the mentee – for it is a poem of dualities and neurotic urges (Horney described them as two horses pulling in opposite directions). That explains all the "me" eye-rhymes. It's a mash-up really of Yeats's "dancer and the dance" and his "Leda and The Swan" – for there is perhaps no more explosive metaphor for the demonic powers in writing and poetry than those unleashed by the orgiastic tendencies of dance – see Stravinsky (and Lermontov is of course modelled on Nijinsky's lover Diaghilev). So, it seems a simple brief poem but it also ghosted by The Ballets Russes, and Stravinsky's "Rite of Spring" choreography, which, when first performed in 1913 is said to have prefigured The Great War and the rise of Modernism.'

GEORGE SZIRTES is the author of some fifteen books of poetry and roughly the same of translation from Hungarian. His first, *The Slant Door* (1979) was joint winner of the Faber Memorial Prize. In 2004 he won the T S Eliot Prize for *Reel*, and was shortlisted for the prize again in 2009 for

The Burning of the Books and for *Bad Machine* (2013). Bloodaxe published his *New and Collected Poems* in 2008. In 2013 he was awarded major prizes both for translation and for his book of poems for children, In the Land of Giants.

He writes, '"Sealed with a Kiss" is one of a series of sonnets based on YouTube clips of old hits. Here is the link https://www.youtube.com/watch?v=xIkUiD8N81k In selecting this clip and the others I wasn't interested in production values or even musical quality but in qualities that had taken on a faintly haunting aspect.

'The singer, Bryan Hyland, was briefly a "teen idol" whose music, as Wikipedia has it, was "puppy-love pop [that] virtually defined the sound and sensibility of bubblegum during the pre-Beatles era." I'd have been no more than thirteen at the time the song first appeared. Now I am trying to understand what I would barely have understood then. In any case, it seems to me that the project of understanding is one of the vital concerns of poetry.

'The poem is not an attempt to reproduce the song or its effect. It isn't *ekphrasis* by other means. It is about of state of mind, state of affairs, state of place. What was the yearning about? What is it to feel yearning as the song seems to feel it?

'In formal terms the poem is a sonnet, that is to say it is in one of those received forms that has been so beaten about it can do practically anything that suggests development under concentrated and compressed conditions. It is a space with echoes from here, there, and everywhere. I have lived with it a long time, though less so recently, but its chosen imperatives of proportion, register and rhyme act jointly as an invitation to invention and an incentive to explore the half-known unknown.'

REBECCA TAMÁS was born in London and currently lives in Norwich, where she is studying for a PhD in Creative and Critical Writing at The University of East Anglia. Her first pamphlet of poetry, *The Ophelia Letters*, was published by Salt in 2013 and was included in *Sabotage Review*'s Top Ten Poetry Books Of The Year. She is currently working on her first collection, and a thesis that addresses ecological poetry and Adorno's theory of the non-identical.

She writes, 'This poem came out of a long held obsession with the filmmaker Werner Herzog: the thrilling originality of his work, and the utter, uncompromising oddness of his personality. Herzog is an almost mythical figure to me in his refusal to think, or live, in a way prescribed by the mainstream film industry or indeed society in general. Herzog does not do "normal." Rather he travels across continents, making bizarre, challenging and beautiful films that reveal to us the unexpected wonder and terror that exist under the surface of everyday reality. Herzog's artistic project is a refusal of both banality and transcendence, instead focusing on the infinite strangeness of our material and psychological world, its unpredictable changeability and flux. It is this vivid, shifting strangeness that I believe can also be accessed in poetry, and which I aim to locate within my work. This poem dramatises the way that Herzog has influenced my understanding of art's potential, imagining what it would mean to be able to follow his example completely, in life and in the imagination: the sacrifice of normality and safety, the revelation of a huge, daunting reality that does not provide easily comprehensible meaning, but which offers the opportunity for transformation.'

PHILIP TERRY is currently Director of Creative Writing at the University of Essex. He is the editor of the story anthology *Ovid Metamorphosed*, author of the poetry collections *Oulipoems*, *Oulipoems 2*, *Shakespeare's Sonnets* and *Advanced Immorality*, and translator of works by Raymond Queneau and Georges Perec. His novel tapestry was shortlisted for the 2013 Goldsmiths Prize. *Dante's Inferno* was published by Carcanet in 2014.

He writes, 'Translating Dante again, especially the *Inferno*, given the wealth of recent translations, calls for some explanation. When that translation involves shifting the action from the twelfth to the twentieth and twenty-first centuries, and relocating it to Essex University, some explanation is all the more urgent. One starting point was architectural: the walled cities of the Italian city-states in the middle ages, typified by Montereggione with its fourteen high towers, to which Dante makes allusion in Canto XXXI, and which underpin the iconography of the *Inferno*, also underpin the architecture of Essex University, where a number of towers surround a central campus, divided up into squares modelled on Italian *campi* (the origin of our modern word "campus"). Another was psychogeographical, taking its cue from the revisioning mappings of the situationists and of writers and artists such as Rebecca Solnit and Jorge Macchi, and involved the palimpsestic strategy of superimposing a map of one place (here Dante's *Inferno*) on another (Essex University and its environs). As the work proceeded, the two maps, by twists and turns, sometimes guided by instinct, sometimes by unpredictable coincidences, began to converge more and more: Dante's Phlegethon, the river of blood, became the river Colne; his popes were replaced by vice-chancellors and, at the suggestion of Robert Sheppard, David Willetts; his suicides, whose souls are reborn as the seeds of trees, became the trees planted to commemorate untimely student deaths on the Essex campus; the warring Guelfs and Ghibellines of Dante's Florence were replaced by the sectarians of Belfast, my home city; and Virgil, finally, was replaced by one-time Essex visiting professor Ted Berrigan, who, like the Latin poet, had imagined the underworld in his poem "Memorial Day": "I heard the dead, the city dead/The devils that surround us". By replacing the historical figures in Dante with our contemporaries I hope to have dispensed with the need for extensive footnotes, while remaining faithful to the spirit and integrity of Dante's text.'

HELEN TOOKEY is a poet and editor. Born near Leicester in 1969, she now lives in Liverpool. Her first full-length poetry collection, *Missel-Child*, was published by Carcanet in 2014 and has been selected by New Writing North for the 2015 "Read Regional" promotion.

She writes, 'The text for this poem came from a book I picked up in a charity shop called *Along the Roman Roads*, by G.M. Boumphrey, published in 1935. The Fosse Way was one of the main Roman roads, running in an almost completely straight line from Exeter to Lincoln, through Bath, Cirencester, and Leicester (where I grew up). I enjoy the way that this kind of collage or cut-up technique can result in a text that's suggestive without ever quite resolving into a clear meaning. This poem is part of an occasional series of attempts to tackle the issue facing everyone who comes from the Midlands: that of coming from a place that's often seen as a no-place, a space-between.'

JACK UNDERWOOD was born in Norwich in 1984. He graduated from Norwich School of Art and Design in 2005 before completing an MA and PhD in Creative Writing at Goldsmiths College, where he now teaches English Literature and Creative Writing. He won an Eric Gregory Award in 2007 and Faber published his debut pamphlet in October 2009 as part of the Faber New Poet series. He also teaches at the Poetry School, co-edits the anthology series *Stop Sharpening Your Knives*, and reviews for *Poetry London* and *Poetry Review*. His debut collection *Happiness* will be published by Faber in 2015.

He writes, 'The poem is a bit of a cheap trick, really, in the sense that it sets up these symbols, these things that seem significant, which draw you into finding possible connections or associations, but then the ending just eradicates all of this imaginative work in a couple of sentences. I suppose that shocks the reader, but I want the process to bring them into a tangibly clear space at the end, to just be left, via the speaker, with just themselves to consider. I think I steal a lot from Bishop's "The Waiting Room", though this only occurred to me some time after publishing it. It's not based on anything I've experienced in my life exactly, though I have climbed a hill and I suppose that like most people, I'm a liar.'

KATE WAKELING was born in Yorkshire and lives in London. She is an ethnomusicologist by training, studying music at Cambridge University and completing a PhD about Balinese gamelan music at the School of

Oriental and African Studies. She is currently a research fellow at Trinity Laban Conservatoire of Music and Dance and writer-in-residence with Aurora Orchestra, where she writes verse and stories for children's concerts.

She writes, '"Riddle" was partly sparked by a poem called "The Englishman's Catechism" by Peter Davidson. As its title suggests, Davidson's poem uses a question-and-answer format, which struck me as a brilliant and intriguing way to unpick ideas in a poem. I also wanted to think about this opaque and slightly provoking relationship I seem to have with music-making, where I'm often trying to creep away from it but somehow it always finds a way to creep up on me. I sometimes find myself thinking of music as a belligerent and faintly menacing beast looming in my peripherals, so decided to probe this creature a bit more, exploring what sorts of properties it might have and imagining how it might respond to some questioning. I also liked the idea of music being a kind of riddle, full of buried sense that is at once fugitive while also being almost embarrassingly obvious. It seems that quite a few other people have since consistently solved the riddle in another, quite different way and with an answer which seems to hold a more material (and dare I say quaint) meaning than I would likely have intended in such a thing, but that admittedly makes a much crisper sense of it all. Which is just the sort of trick I suspect music likes playing.'

MARK WALDRON was born in New York. His first collection, *The Brand New Dark*, was published by Salt in 2008, his second, *The Itchy Sea*, came out in September 2011. His work appears in *Identity Parade: New British and Irish Poets* (Bloodaxe 2010) and *Best British Poetry 2012* and *2013*, both published by Salt.

He writes, 'Personally I'm attached to this poem though I'm always surprised when other people say they like it. The first time I recited it at a reading I introduced it as a kind of nonsense poem so that if people didn't get much sense out of it at least they'd think that was my intention. I was being dishonest, it's not really a nonsense poem, although I'm aware it's a bit elusive.

'The poem mostly consists of a series of images that the voice in the poem is inviting someone to consider. The first is something he has produced from his imagination – the bespoke rabbit folk emerging from their squiggly silos, the next is the way he sees his relationship to his body, his *consort bod*; then he talks about how he relates to the person we realise he's addressing, as he leafs so slowly through her autonomous scent; and then he describes the way he pictures the world and himself in it. They're not particularly connected images and there is one which I really can't explain at all – *I fill myself also, like a dog fills its wallop.*

It's there because it just seems or sounds true to me. I'm pretty sure it does mean something (I don't really believe in the existence of nonsense generated by a person); it's just that I'm not sure exactly what it is that it means.

'In the last line I think the voice in the poem means to express how very badly he wants to be touched. I love the ending of the James Wright poem: *Lying in a Hammock at William Duffy's Farm in Pine Island*, Minnesota, when he suddenly says, *I have wasted my life*. I know it's meant as an epiphany, but I've always imagined it as bursting out of him – as the only thing he really wanted to say. I hoped the last line in this poem might have some of that effect.'

SARAH WARDLE was educated at the universities of Oxford and Sussex and has a first-class BA, MA and D.Phil.. She has won *Poetry Review*'s Geoffrey Dearmer Award and been shortlisted for Forward Best First Collection. She had been poet in residence for Bedgbury National Pinetum, Tottenham Hotspur Football Club, the British Council in Berlin and Transport for London at Embankment Station, and has been Royal Literary Fund Fellow at Royal Holloway. She is a lecturer at Morley College and Lecturer in Poetry at Middlesex University. Her books are *Fields Away* (2003), *Score!* (2005), *A Knowable World* (2009) and *Beyond* (2014).

She writes, 'This sonnet celebrates being free and at liberty to enjoy London life. Its form is tight, yet at the same time overspilling and all in one sentence, showing the ongoing energy of the metropolis 24/7. It harks back to ideas of the freedman of ancient Rome, as well as the freedom of the city of London, and is informed by the author's experience of having been deprived of liberty over a dozen times as an inpatient for mental health treatment. Here the iambic pentameter becomes the heartbeat pulse of the city and the multiplicity of people in it. It is a poem which celebrates humanity, the present and looks forward to life going on in others" experience after each person's single death. In this it celebrates a secular afterlife, a London "Beyond" one's own experience, to take the title of the collection from which it is taken. It encapsulates hope and positivity, a reason for being alive and belonging to the diversity of a vibrant city as an argument for not despairing and giving in to depression and self-pity, which the whole book, Beyond, is a journey past and on from. This poem is central to the awakening of the whole book, coming towards the end of the collection and representing a progression from the bleaker poems of the start, as new life, love and hope have been attained through the individual poem's narrative.'

SARAH WESTCOTT's debut pamphlet *Inklings* (Flipped Eye) was a winner of the Venture Poetry Award and the Poetry Book Society's Pamphlet

Choice for Winter 2013. Her poems have been published in magazines including *Poetry Review*, *Magma* and *Poetry Wales*, anthologies including *Days of Roses* and *Where Rockets Burn Through* (Penned in the Margins), and on beer mats. Sarah lives with her family on the London/Kent borders and earns a living as a journalist.

She writes, '"Messenger" was one of those rare poems that came to me quite quickly and fairly well-formed, as if it was waiting to be heard and set down. I wrote the first draft long-hand in Starbucks, on the edge of a bit of newspaper, while on a work break from writing about celebrities. I've always appreciated the arrival of swifts in our urban spaces every summer – their crescent bows and their eerie, wild screams.

'I think the poem has its roots in childhood – my Dad and I would sometimes walk the Devon lanes in the twilight, and one evening we found a swift, grounded. I remember picking it up, and how fragile and otherworldly it felt in our hands. I had been trying to write about this encounter for some years and made several attempts before deciding to move away from the bird itself, and towards a more multivalent and ambiguous interpretation.

'I was inspired by the god Mercury, the tradition of angelic messengers, and the language of sailing which might capture something of the interface between human and air. A place that humans can only temporarily occupy.

'"To set away, windward" suggests, for me, the idea of "letting go" into something bigger than oneself. I hope this poem can be interpreted in multiple ways.'

SAM WILLETTS was born in 1962. He read English at Wadham College, Oxford. He has worked as a journalist and a teacher, as well as having had many more or less menial jobs. His first collection, *New Light For The Old Dark* (Cape Poetry 2010) was shortlisted for five major awards including the 2010 T.S. Eliot Prize; he is a also a former winner of the Bridport Prize for poetry. He lives in Cheltenham with two cats and is working on a second collection.

He writes, '"Caravaggio" was very hard to write with honesty, and self-honesty. The question of one's own true part in things is very important in (my) recovery from addiction, and from dishonest living,. The poem describes how a paedophile picked me up and took me to his home. In trying to be honest, I came up against various obstacles: my "mythologising" of the event, my shame about what did/didn't happen, how I truly felt about it, then and now. I worried that it wasn't "bad" enough – I wasn't raped or hurt – and wondered whether I was making my role more passive than it really was, and so less shaming. I hope I have conveyed my ambivalence at the time, which preceded – which caused, I think – the murderous rage I felt just hours later. I didn't want the poem to present me as merely a pathetic victim, and had to remind myself – still do – that my eventual complicity (the guy had his seduction routiine down perfectly) didn't justify his actions. It's tricky – hence the poem I suppose. I hope I've put across the context, of truanting, waste places, the murky margins, vividly.'

HUGO WILLIAMS was born in Windsor in 1942 and grew up in Sussex. From 1961 to 1970 he worked on the *London Magazine*. He has been TV critic and poetry editor of the *New Statesman* and poetry editor of the *Spectator*, and for two decades contributed the 'Freelance' column to the *TLS*. He has published 12 collections of poems, the most recent of which is *I Knew the Bride* (2014). *Billy's Rain* was awarded the T.S. Eliot Prize in 1999. The poems selected here are part of a sequence about his experience of receiving dialysis treatment for kidney failure, diagnosed in 2011. In an interview published in the Spring 2014 edition of *Poetry Review*, Williams commented: 'Writing has always been a natural thing for me to do, the only thing which inspired my energy. With the dialysis poems, I needed them so badly because I was so oppressed by this terrible fate.'

JOHN HARTLEY WILLIAMS was born in 1942 in Cheshire and grew up in London. He studied at Nottingham University and later at the University of London. From 1976 until his death in May 2014 he lived in Berlin. He published nine collections of poetry, two of which were shortlisted for the T.S. Eliot Prize. He also published translations from German, French, Serbo-Croatian as well as versions of the Rumanian poet Marin Sorescu. A reader-friendly guide to the writing of poetry called *Teach Yourself Writing Poetry*, co-written with the Irish poet Matthew Sweeney, was reissued in a revised edition by Hodder in 2004.

WILLIAM WOOTTEN was born in 1971. He grew up in Somerset and studied at the Universities of Cambridge, Edinburgh and Durham. He has done a range of jobs and now lectures in English at the University of Bristol. His essays and book reviews have appeared widely and his critical study, *The Alvarez Generation* is due from Liverpool University Press in 2015. Poems of his have appeared in magazines including *PN Review*, *Poetry Review*, *The Spectator* and the *Times Literary Supplement*.

He writes, 'Any poem which conceals a debt to the John Landis movie *Trading Places* isn't going to be entirely about the early sixteenth century. Still, the setting for "The Harvest" is Wittenberg at around the time of the Reformation, Wittenberg being of course the city in which Martin Luther produced his Ninety-Five Theses and where tradition says he nailed them to the door of the Castle Church. Wittenberg is also the city best-associated with Luther's contemporary, the magician and alchemist Johann Georg Faust, the man who was quickly to be turned into the legendary figure the English would know as Dr. Faustus. According to stories that gave rise to the early Faust Book, Faustus summoned Mephistopheles and signed a contract in his own blood. This contract promised Faustus's own immortal soul in return for his having his bidding done for the period of twenty-four years. During these twenty-four years, *Faustus* took advantage of the ability to transform his appearance, command evil spirits and conjure up comestibles in order to drink good wine, make easy money and play tricks upon the unsuspecting. These few details, and that Faustus had an apprentice named Wagner, are all the reader might need to know to follow the narrative of "The Harvest", for while it hadn't escaped my notice that some of the most celebrated works of German and English literature had got at the Faustus legend before I did, I found it much more convenient to write "The Harvest" as if they hadn't.'

LIST OF MAGAZINES

3:AM Magazine,
www.3ammagazine.com/3am/
Editor-in-Chief: Andrew Gallix
Poetry Editor: S.J. Fowler

Ambit, Staithe House, Main Road,
Brancaster Staithe, Norfolk,
PE31 8BP
Editor: Briony Bax
Poetry Editors: Liz
Berry, Declan Ryan

Areté, 8 New College
Lane, Oxford, OX1 3BN
United Kingdom
Editor: Craig Raine

Days of Roses, http://
daysofroses.wordpress.com
Editors: Declan Ryan and
Malene Engelund,

Edinburgh Review, 22a Buccleuch
Place, Edinburgh EH8 9LN

Granta 12 Addison Avenue
London W11 4QR
Editor: Sigrid Rausing

Kaffeeklatsch manualpoetry.co.uk/
Editors: Matthew Halliday, Nadia
Connor and Joey Connolly

Lighthouse Georgian House 34
Thoroughfare, Halesworth,
Suffolk, IP19 8AP
Editor: Andrew McDonnell

The London Review of Books
London Review of Books, 28
Little Russell Street, London
WC1A 2HN, edit@lrb.co.uk

Magma, www.magmapoetry.com/
23 Pine Walk, Carshalton
SM5 4ES

The Manchester Review, Centre
for New Writing, Second Floor,
Mansfield Cooper Building, The
University of Manchester, Oxford
Road, Manchestser, M13 9PL
Editor: John McAuliffe

The New Statesman 7th Floor
John Carpenter House, 7
Carmelite Street, Blackfriars,
London EC4Y 0AN
Editor: Jason Cowley

New Walk newwalkmagazine.
wordpress.com
Editor: Rory Waterman

The Pickled Body
thepickledbody.tumblr.com
Editors: Dimitra Xidous
and Patrick Chapman

PN Review, Dept. of English,
University of Glasgow,
5 University Gardens,
Glasgow, G12 8QH
Editor: Michael Schmidt

Poem c/o Durham University,
Department of English Studies
Hallgarth House, 77 Hallgarth
Street, Durham City DH1 3AY
Editor: Fiona Sampson

Poem in Which poemsinwhich.
wordpress.com
Editors: Amy Key and Nia Davies

Poetry London, 81 Lambeth
Walk, London SE11 6DX
Editor: Ahren Warner

Poetry Proper , www.
poetryproper.blogspot.co.uk
Editors: Miriam Gamble, Paul
Maddern and Alex Wylie

Poetry Review, The Poetry
Society, 22 Betterton Street,
London, WC2H 9BX

Poetry Wales, 57 Nolton Street,
Bridgend, Wales, CF31 3AE UK
Editor: Zoë Skoulding

The Rialto, PO Box 309,
Aylesham, Norwich NR11 6LN
Editor: Michael Mackmin

Shearsman, 58 Velwell
Road, Exeter, EX4 4LD
Editor: Tony Frazer

Times Literary Supplement
3 Thomas More Square,
London E98 1BS
Poetry Editor: Alan Jenkins

The White Review, www.
thewhitereview.org
8th Floor, 1 Knightsbridge
Green, London SW1X 7QA
Editors: Benjamin Eastham and
Jacques Testard

ACKNOWLEDGEMENTS

Grateful acknowledgement is made to the publications from which the poems in this volume were chosen. Unless specifically noted otherwise, copyright to the poems is held by the individual poets.

Mir Mahfuz Ali: 'MIG-21 Raids at Shegontola' appeared in *Poetry Review*. and was collected in *Midnight, Dhaka* (Seren, 2014). Reprinted by permission of the poet and the publisher.

Rachael Allen: 'Science and Math' appeared in *Poetry London* and was collected in *Faber New Poets 9* (Faber & Faber 2014) Reprinted by permission of the poet and the publisher.

Robert Anthony: 'Clouds' appeared in *Kaffeeklatsch*. Reprinted by permission of the poet.

Simon Armitage: 'Emergency' appeared in *The New Statesman*. Reprinted by permission of the poet.

Michael Bayley: 'Estuary' appeared in *Poetry Wales*. Reprinted by permission of the poet.

Fiona Benson: 'Toboggan Run' appeared in *Granta* and was collected in *Bright Travellers* (Cape, 2014). Reprinted by permission of the poet and the publishers.

Emily Berry: 'Picnic' appeared in *Granta*. Reprinted by permission of the poet.

Liz Berry: 'Scenes from The Passion – The First Path' appeared in *Poetry Review*. Reprinted by permission of the poet.

Rachael Boast: 'The North Porch' appeared in *Edinburgh Review* and collected in *Pilgrim's Flower* (Picador, 2014). Reprinted by permission of the poet and the publisher.

Alan Brownjohn: 'Index of First Lines' appeared in the *Times Literary Supplement*. Reprinted by permission of the poet.

Colette Bryce: 'Don't speak to the Brits, just pretend they don't exist' appeared in *Edinburgh Review* and was collected in *The Whole & Rain-Domed Universe* (Picador, 2014). Reprinted by permission of the poet and the publisher.

John Burnside: 'Choir' appeared in the *London Review of Books* and collected in *All One Breath* (Cape, 2014). Reprinted by permission of the poet and the publisher.

Dominic Bury: 'A Prism of Signs' appeared in *Poetry Wales*. Reprinted by permission of the poet.

Anthony Caleshu: from 'The Victor Poems' appeared in *The Manchester Review*. Reprinted by permission of the poet.

Geraldine Clarkson: 'The thing about Grace and Laura' appeared in *Shearsman*. Reprinted by permission of the poet.

Sophie Collins: 'Desk' appeared in *Poetry London*. Reprinted by permission of the poet.

Joey Connolly: 'Chekhov's Gun' appeared in *Poems in Which*. Reprinted by permission of the poet.

Siân Melangell Dafydd: 'Big Cats' appeared in *Poetry Wales*. Reprinted by permission of the poet.

Joe Dresner: 'a glass of ice cold milk' appeared in *Kaffeeklatsch*. Reprinted by permission of the poet.

Laura Elliott: 'Skype Blinks' appeared in *3:AM Magazine*. Reprinted by permission of the poet.

Malene Engelund: 'The Terns'appeared in *Days of Roses*. Reprinted by permission of the poet.

Richard Evans: 'Space Invader' appeared in *Magma*. Reprinted by permission of the poet.

Ruth Fainlight: 'The Motorway' appeared in *Poem*. Reprinted by permission of the poet.

Matthew Francis: 'Silverfish, Moth' appeared in *Poetry Review*. Reprinted by permission of the poet.

Claudia Friedrich: 'My Disseration No Plagiarisation!' appeared in *Kaffeeklatsch*. Reprinted by permission of the poet.

Matthew Gregory: 'A Room at the Grand Hotel des Roches Noires, 1971' appeared in the *London Review of Books*. Reprinted by permission of the poet.

David Harsent: 'Fire: end-scenes and outtakes' appeared in *Poetry London* and was collected in *Fire Songs* (Faber & Faber, 2014). Reprinted by permission of the poet and the publisher.

Lee Harwood: 'The Oak Coffer' appeared in the *London Review of Books*. Reprinted by permission of the poet.

Oli Hazzard: from 'Within Habit' appeared in *Magma*. Reprinted by permission of the poet.

Sarah Howe: 'A loop of jade' appeared in *Poetry London*. Reprinted by permission of the poet.

Caoilinn Hughes: 'Bruisewort' appeared in *Poetry Proper*. Reprinted by permission of the poet.

Kirsten Irving: 'No Fish Are We Now' appeared in *The New Statesman*. Reprinted by permission of the poet.

Alan Jenkins: 'Deptford' appeared in *New Walk*. Reprinted by permission of the poet.

Mimi Khalvati: 'Bringing Down the Stars' appeared in *The Rialto*. and was collected in *The Weather Wheel* (Carcanet, 2014). Reprinted by permission of the poet and the publisher.

Hannah Lowe: 'The Other Family' appeared in *Kaffeeklatsch*. Reprinted by permission of the poet.

Lydia MacPherson: 'Lithium Lovesong' appeared in *Days of Roses*. Reprinted by permission of the poet.

Glyn Maxwell: 'Modu and Mahu' appeared in *Poetry London*. Reprinted by permission of the poet.

Chris McCabe: 'The Duchess of Malfi' appeared in *Poetry London*. Reprinted by permission of the poet.

Christopher Middleton: 'Go With Isaac Rosenberg' appeared in *Poetry London*. Reprinted by permission of the poet.

Andrew Motion: 'The Mill' appeared in the *Times Literary Supplement*. Reprinted by permission of the poet.

André Naffis-Sahely: 'Through the Rockies' appeared in *Areté*. Reprinted by permission of the poet.

John North: 'Summer Solstice, Cumbria' appeared in *Kaffeeklatsch*. Reprinted by permission of the poet.

Ruth Padel: 'The Chain' appeared in *Poetry London* and was collected in *Learning to Make an Oud in Nazareth* (Chatto & Windus, 2014). Reprinted by permission of the poet and the publisher.

Abigail Parry: 'Girl to Snake' appeared in *Poems In Which*. Reprinted by permission of the poet.

Christopher Riesco: 'Caliban Life' appeared in *Kaffeeklatsch*. Reprinted by permission of the poet.

Carol Rumens: 'Easter Snow' appeared in *The Rialto*. Reprinted by permission of the poet.

Declan Ryan: 'Ethiopia Shall Stretch Forth Her Hands' appeared in *Poetry London*. Reprinted by permission of the poet.

Richard Scott: 'Pilgrimage' appeared in *Magma*. Reprinted by permission of the poet.

Ian Seed: 'Prize-Giving' appeared in *PN Review* and collected in *Makers of Empty Dreams* (Shearsman Books, 2014). Reprinted by permission of the poet and the publisher.

Martha Sprackland: 'Dooms' appeared in the *London Review of Books*. Reprinted by permission of the poet.

Julian Stannard: 'September 1939' appeared in *Ambit* and was collected in *The Street of Perfect Love* (Worple Press, 2014). Reprinted by permission of the poet and the publisher.

Jon Stone: 'Endings to Adventure Gamebooks 22' appeared in *The New Statesman*. Reprinted by permission of the poet.

Todd Swift: 'Red Shoes' appeared in *The Pickled Body*. Reprinted by permission of the poet.

George Szirtes: 'Sealed With a Kiss' appeared in *3:AM Magazine*. Reprinted by permission of the poet.

Rebecca Tamás: 'A Trip With Werner Herzog' appeared in *Kaffeeklatsch*. Reprinted by permission of the poet.

Philip Terry: 'Inferno: Canto I' appeared in the *London Review of Books*. and was collected in *Dante's Inferno* (Carcanet, 2014). Reprinted by permission of the poet amnd the publisher.

Helen Tookey: 'Fosse Way' appeared in *Poetry Review* and collected in *Missel-Child* (Carcanet, 2014). Reprinted by permission of the poet and the publisher.

Jack Underwood: 'Thank you for your email' appeared in *The White Review*. Reprinted by permission of the poet.

Mark Waldron: 'First off,' appeared in *Poetry London*. Reprinted by permission of the poet.

Kate Wakeling: 'Riddle' appeared in *The Rialto*. Reprinted by permission of the poet.

Sarah Wardle: 'Freeman' appeared in *Poetry Review*. Reprinted by permission of the poet.

Sarah Westcott: 'Messenger' appeared in *Poetry Review*. Reprinted by permission of the poet.

Sam Willetts: 'Caravaggio' appeared in *Poetry Review*. Reprinted by permission of the poet.

Hugo Williams: from 'Notes from Dialysis' appeared in *Poetry Review*. Reprinted by permission of the poet.

John Hartley Williams: 'I Inspect the Storm' appeared in the *London Review of Books*. Reprinted by permission of the poet.

William Wootten: 'The Harvest' appeared in *New Walk*. Reprinted by permission of the poet.

ALSO AVAILABLE
FROM SALT

POETRY

Best British Poetry 2011 (9781907773044),
series edited by Roddy Lumsden

Best British Poetry 2012 (9781907773259),
series edited by Roddy Lumsden, guest editor Sascha Dugdale

Best British Poetry 2013 (9781907773556),
series edited by Roddy Lumsden, guest editor Ahren Warner

The Salt Book of Younger Poets (9781907773105),
edited by Roddy Lumsden and Eloise Stonborough

SHORT STORIES

Best British Short Stories 2011 (9781907773129),
edited by Nicholas Royle

Best British Short Stories 2012 (9781907773181),
edited by Nicholas Royle

Best British Short Stories 2013 (9781907773471),
edited by Nicholas Royle

Best British Short Stories 2014 (9781907773679),
edited by Nicholas Royle

ALSO AVAILABLE
FROM SALT

ELIZABETH BAINES
Too Many Magpies (9781844717217)
The Birth Machine (9781907773020)

LESLEY GLAISTER
Little Egypt (9781907773723)

ALISON MOORE
The Lighthouse (9781907773174)
The PreWar House and Other Stories (9781907773501)
He Wants (9781907773815)

ALICE THOMPSON
Justine (9781784630324)
The Falconer (9781784630096)
The Existential Detective (9781784630119)
Burnt Island (9781907773488)

MEIKE ZIERVOGEL
Magda (9781907773402)
Clara's Daughter (9781907773792)

NEXT GENERATION
POETS AT SALT
